Real Talk Becoming Who God Made You to Be

A Christian Guide for Teen Boys on Confidence, Identity, and Faith

Dr. Scott Fuller

Ivory Road Resources

Real Talk: Becoming Who God Made You to Be — A Christian Guide for Teen Boys on Confidence, Identity, and Faith
Part of The Real Talk Series

Published by **Ivory Road Resources**
www.ivoryroad.shop

Printed in the United States of America

ISBN:

Paperback: 978-1-970494-05-1

First Edition, 2026

Contents

Author's Note

This guide was created with one goal in mind: to help you walk alongside students as they discover who they are and who God made them to be. Leading teens in honest conversations about faith is not always easy. But your presence, your questions, and your steady encouragement matter more than you know.

This book was developed with the help of AI tools to organize ideas, sharpen drafts, and shape content clearly. The message, though, comes from real life, real faith, and real conversations with students, parents, and leaders over many years.

Thank you for investing your time, heart, and energy in the next generation. You are doing sacred work, even on the hard days.

With gratitude,

Scott

Dedication

To every middle school student I had the honor of pastoring—

Guys and girls, your energy, questions, struggles, and joy helped shape this book more than you'll ever know.
You showed me how deeply these years matter.
Thank you for letting me walk part of your journey.

And for Matthew—

My amazing nephew, whose heart, humor, and honesty inspired these pages.
I believe in you. I see the calling on your life.
And I can't wait to see how God uses you.
You are the reason this book has a name.

—Uncle Scott

Introduction

This book is for the guys who feel like they have to be strong all the time, but secretly feel weak. For the ones who make people laugh, but cry when they're alone. For the student who gets good grades, but still feels like a failure. For the athlete, the gamer, the quiet one, the leader, the doubter, the young man who wonders, What's wrong with me?

Here's the answer: Nothing. You're not broken. You're growing into the person you were made to be.

Let's be honest: most books aren't written for guys like you. They're either too boring, too preachy, or so full of fluff you forget what they were even trying to say. This isn't one of those books. I didn't create it to impress anybody. I created it because I remember being where you are, and I know how long those years can feel when you're carrying something you can't name.

That question, Am I enough, is where Real Talk begins. And I don't want you to go through these years thinking you're the only one asking it. Because you're not. This is the book I needed then. Before I learned that the questions I was carrying weren't weakness. They were the beginning of something. Now it's yours.

This book won't give you all the answers, but it will help you ask the right questions. It's full of real talk: stories, Scripture, practical tools, and moments where you might laugh, cry, or just say, "Yeah... same." Each chapter tackles something real: confidence, identity, friendship, faith, fear, purpose. You'll have space to reflect, tools to try, and no pressure to get it all right.

This book won't fix your life, but it might help you live it differently. So here's my challenge: be honest with yourself, with God, with someone you trust. Let down your walls, just for a moment, and let these pages speak to the part of you that's tired of pretending. Because change is possible. Growth is real. And the fact that you picked up this book? That tells me you're ready.

You don't have to figure all of this out alone. Along the way, you'll find extra tools, reflection resources, and conversation guides created to help you keep growing beyond these pages. Some are included in the Real Talk series, and others are available free at www.ivoryroad.shop.

Turn the page. Let's start with the mirror.

PART I – WHO AM I, REALLY?

Seeing Yourself Clearly: Identity, Self-Worth & Confidence

You ever look in the mirror and feel like you're staring at a stranger? Some days you like the guy looking back. Other days, you can't stop noticing everything you wish you could change. ***And then there's the version you show the world***, the guy who laughs at the right times, acts like nothing bothers him, and hides the stuff that actually does.

That's the thing about these years, they can feel like one big competition. Who's the funniest. Who's the strongest. Who gets noticed first. And every time you start to feel okay about yourself, you catch a glimpse of someone else and think, *Why can't I be more like him?*

Comparison will steal from you if you let it. It'll twist your view of yourself until you forget the truth: you were never made to be someone else. You were made to be you.

God's been saying that since the beginning. *"You are God's masterpiece. He created you to do good things He planned long ago"* (Ephesians 2:10).

You're not an accident. You're not a backup plan. You were designed on purpose, with purpose.

So, this part of the book? It's about finding that guy again—the one God made you to be. No filters. No fake confidence. **Just you**, learning to see yourself the way He already does.

Chapter One

The Mirror Lies Sometimes

Learning to See Yourself Through Truth, Not Insecurity

Do you ever stand in front of a mirror and not *like* the guy looking back at you? Not because you've got toothpaste on your shirt or bedhead you can't tame. I'm talking about those quiet moments when you stare at your reflection and think, *"This isn't who I'd like to see. This isn't the version of me I wanted to be."*

I've had plenty of those moments. Middle school. High school. Even after that. There were mornings I'd wake up, crawl out of the bed, and head to the bathroom only to see a person staring back who didn't feel like me at all. Shoulders slouched. Eyes tired. Expression flat. Like even my face had given up trying.

From the outside, things looked fine. I had friends, decent grades, nothing majorly wrong. But inside? **I felt like a fraud.**

It wasn't one big failure that made me feel that way. There wasn't some dramatic moment that crushed my confidence. It was quieter than that—more like a whisper that wouldn't go away:

"You're not strong enough. "You're just pretending." "Everyone else has it figured out—you don't."

The weird thing? That whisper was so soft no one else could hear it—but it was loud enough to drown out every compliment, every achievement, every moment someone told me they were proud of me.

I'd smile in the hallway and laugh with friends, but when I was alone, especially in front of a mirror, *it felt like I was staring at a stranger.* Like I was trying to show up to life as someone else and couldn't quite pull it off.

And I didn't tell anyone. Not my friends. Not my parents. Not even God—not really. Because how do you explain something you can't even name? *So I kept it buried, carrying that quiet heaviness everywhere I went—until it started shaping how I saw myself.*

It wasn't until I stopped trying to fix the reflection and started listening to a different voice that anything actually changed.

But why do we feel this way in the first place?

Here's what I've learned: insecurity doesn't need an invitation. Sometimes it sneaks in like fog, settling so slowly you don't notice until everything feels blurry. Other times it comes in like a punch to the gut—a joke, a comparison, a post online that makes you wish you were someone else.

Either way, it rewrites your story. Slowly. Quietly. Until you're reading a version of yourself that was never true.

Looking in the mirror felt like standing in front of one of those carnival mirrors.

At first, you see one flaw—your hair, your body, your smile. But then it spreads, **warping** everything until you hardly recognize the guy staring back.

You start fussing—fixing your hair, adjusting your shirt, even sucking in your stomach—just hoping you'll measure up.

Not to some ruler, but to everyone else. The confident guys who owned every room they walked into. The ones who made it all look effortless.

And every time I came up short, that invisible crack in the mirror grew deeper.

It never spoke, but its silence said everything I didn't have the courage to say out loud.

Here's the thing: **mirrors don't actually lie. They just don't tell the whole truth either.**

And that's where things get tricky.

The glass can only show what's on the outside—your hair, your clothes, your skin. It can't show what's underneath: **your thoughts, your fears, the pressure you feel to always be stronger, cooler, smarter—"enough".**

You can fix your hair a hundred times, but it won't fix that feeling in your chest. You can plaster on the perfect smile, but inside you still feel like you're falling apart.

That's because the real mirror you're looking into isn't hanging on your wall.

It's in your mind.

And that mirror? It doesn't just reflect what's real—it reflects what you ***BELIEVE*** is true. Even when it's a lie.

It's shaped not by facts but by moments:

- Being picked last for a game.
- A comment about your weight.
- A grade that made you feel like a failure.
- A joke that went too far.
- A silence that said more than words ever could.

At first, those moments sting. But if you let them, they sink in and start whispering labels you carry like tattoos:

"You're a failure." "You're ugly." "You're too much." "You're not enough."

And pretty soon, those labels don't just sting—they start to stick. **You begin to *BELIEVE* that's who you are.** After a while, it doesn't feel like you're *feeling* worthless; it feels like you *are* worthless. Like those lies are carved into who you are.

But that's a lie. **A mirror can't define you**. It only reflects what you've been told to focus on. And if all you see are mistakes, flaws, and insecurities, then that's all that shows up in the reflection. But that's not the full story.

If your mirror has been lying to you, it's time to pick up a new one. Not a perfect one. Not a kinder one. A true one. The kind that doesn't lie. The kind of mirror only God can hold up—the one that shows what's always been true about you.

"You are fearfully and wonderfully made." — Psalm 139:14.

You **aren't an accident.** You **aren't a rough draft** God threw together at the last minute. You **aren't made to impress anyone.** You **are made to be real.**

Before you ever saw flaws in the mirror, God saw a *masterpiece.* **Nothing has changed that.**

"Even the hairs of your head are all numbered." — Luke 12:7.

That's how deeply God knows you. Not just the image you see in the mirror or the mask you wear in the hallway, but the real you—the you behind the jokes, the you behind the silence, the you who hides the weight of fear and shame.

God sees it all. And still—**He stays. He loves. He calls you His.**

"Before I formed you in the womb, I knew you." — Jeremiah 1:5.

Think about that. Before you ever took a breath. Before anyone spoke your name. Before you even looked into your first mirror—**God knew you. And He chose you.**

That truth is bigger than any label you've been given. **Stronger than shame. Louder than lies. Deeper than doubt.**

God's mirror doesn't distort. It doesn't zoom in on your flaws or twist your story. It shows you who you really are—**chosen**, **seen**, **known**, and **loved**.

I once saw this truth play out in the life of a guy named Eli.

Eli was 15. Played JV basketball. Quiet kid. Stayed out of drama. The kind of guy who showed up to practice early, worked hard, and stayed after to shoot free throws when everyone else had gone home.

One day at practice, Eli went up for a layup, got bumped, and tripped. Nothing major—just a fall. Nobody laughed out loud. But someone recorded it.

That night, the clip showed up in the team's group chat. A short loop of Eli hitting the ground. Someone added a dumb sound effect. Another kid made it the group chat photo.

No one apologized. No one said, *"Hey, that's not cool."* Everyone just moved on. Everyone except Eli.

That night, Eli stood in front of his bathroom mirror replaying it over and over—not just the fall, but the silence. The way nobody had his back. The way it felt like he was a joke to the whole team.

On the outside, nothing had changed. Same brown hair. Same hoodie. Same tired eyes. But inside? **He felt small. Embarrassed. Like he didn't belong.**

He didn't tell anyone. Not his parents. Not his coach. Not even his youth pastor.

But that weekend at youth group, something shifted. The leader gave a message about identity—about how the world throws labels at us and how some of those labels stick, even though God never meant for us to carry them.

Eli didn't raise his hand. Didn't say a word. But something clicked.

That night when he got home, he went to his room, grabbed a sticky note, and wrote six simple words: *"I am* ***more*** *than they think."*

He stuck it to the corner of his mirror. Not because everything was magically okay. Not because he suddenly felt confident. Not because the hurt disappeared.

But because, somewhere deep down, **he chose to believe something else: *that God's voice mattered more than the team's group chat.***

The next day, Eli showed up to practice. Not because he felt brave. **But because he chose to be brave.**

Courage isn't always loud. It's not some big speech or dramatic, movie-worthy moment. Sometimes it's a sticky note on your mirror. Sometimes it's just showing up even when you feel small.

Most of the time, courage looks like this: walking back into the room where you felt embarrassed, trying again after everyone saw you fail, refusing to let one mistake or one label define your whole story.

That's what Eli did. And that's what you can do, too.

Because here's the truth: **you don't have to feel brave to *be* brave.** Bravery isn't about suddenly becoming fearless. It's about trusting that God's truth about you is louder than fear.

Even when the mirror screams lies. Even when you feel broken or invisible. Even when your chest feels heavy and you don't know what to say.

You can choose **courage**. You can choose **truth.**

And here's the good news: **God doesn't wait for you to get it all *together* before He meets you.** He doesn't wait for you to stand tall, smile wide, or fix every flaw.

He meets you right there—**right in the middle of your fear—and whispers: *"I know you. I made you. I love you. I'm not leaving."***

That's the moment everything changes. Not when the hurt goes away. When you decide whose voice gets the final word. So, what do you do when the mirror lies to you like that?

You start by noticing the lies. When that inner voice whispers *"You're not enough,"* pause. Name it for what it is: **a lie.** Don't shove it down or try to out-shout it. Just stop and call it out: *"This isn't the truth about me."*

Then, trace it back. Ask yourself: *Where did this come from?* Was it a comment someone made? A moment you've never forgotten? A habit of comparing yourself to everyone else? When you trace a lie back to its source, it loses some of its power. It's not wisdom. It's a wound someone left behind.

Next, replace it with God's truth. Say it out loud if you have to:

"I am loved." "I'm not alone." "I am becoming who God made me to be." "I don't need to be perfect to have value." "I matter to God—even when I don't feel like it."

Finally, do one small thing that confirms that truth. Write it down. Share it with someone safe. Pray it. Like Eli, tape it to your mirror. Because **the only way to rebuild your reflection is to start reflecting what's real.**

Rebuilding how you see yourself doesn't happen overnight. It starts with small, simple choices. **Here are a few you can try this week:**

- **Speak Truth Out Loud:** Every morning this week, stand in front of your mirror and say Eli's words: *"I am more than they think."* Let your own voice fight the lies.
- **Write Your Own Truth:** Write one truth about who you are in God's eyes and put it somewhere you'll see it your mirror, locker, notebook, or phone lock screen.
- **Quiet the False Mirror:** Take a 24-hour break from comparing yourself to others, whether that's scrolling through social media or replaying harsh words in your head. Instead, ask God, *"What do You see when You look at me?"*
- **Write Your Own Truth:** Write one truth about who you are in God's eyes and put it somewhere you'll see it your mirror, locker, notebook, or phone lock screen.
- **Quiet the False Mirror:** Take a 24-hour break from comparing yourself to others, whether that's scrolling through social media or replaying harsh words in your head. Instead, ask God, *"What do You see when You look at me?"*

You'll still have off days. There will be mornings when you wake up and that old mirror, the one that distorts your reflection, tries to speak again. It might sound like doubt. Or comparison. Or a whisper that says: *"You haven't really changed."*

Don't be surprised when it happens.

Growth doesn't mean the lies go away forever. It means **you've learned how to spot them... and replace them with truth.**

Even on the days you still feel broken or unsure, here's what's different now: **you have a better mirror.**

You've started to rebuild the way you see yourself, not based on what the world says, but on what God says.

And here's what He says:

You are loved.
You are known.
You are chosen.
You are not alone.

You're becoming who God made you to be, not overnight, not all at once, but **one moment, one truth, one step at a time.**

So keep rebuilding that mirror. Keep reflecting what's real. Because now, finally, you're beginning to see what God has seen all along: you are loved, chosen, and becoming who He made you to be. Now that you know the mirror lies, let's talk about who's actually looking back.

Real Talk Mantra: ***The mirror doesn't define you. God does.***

Chapter Two

I'm Not Like Everyone Else (And That's Good)

You weren't made to blend in. You were made to show up. Why your differences aren't just okay—they're powerful.

Sometimes do you feel like you're just not like everyone else—and not in a good way? Maybe it's the way you dress. The way you think. The stuff you actually care about. And it feels like no matter what you do, you're always a little out of step with everyone else.

I'll never forget this moment from sixth grade. Two guys in my class had the exact same backpack. Same brand. Same color. Same zipper pulls. You couldn't tell them apart unless you opened them. One day after school, they accidentally swapped bags. Neither one noticed until halfway home—when one kid reached inside and said, "Wait... this isn't my stuff." The next day, they laughed, traded back, and moved on like nothing happened.

No big deal, right? But then someone made a joke that stuck with me: *"Wouldn't life be easier if we were all the same?"* At the time, I laughed along. But now? I know better.

Being the same might feel easier. But it's **not better**.

If God wanted us to be identical copies of each other, He would've made us that way. But He didn't. He gave each of us different stories, personalities, and gifts **on purpose**.

The problem is, we don't always see our differences as a gift. *We see them as a problem.* We compare ourselves to the people who seem to have it all together, and we start to believe the lie that we have to be more like them to matter.

That's the distortion.

But God's truth says something completely different: *"Do not conform to the pattern of this world, but be transformed by the renewing of your mind."* — Romans 12:2.

You weren't made to blend into whatever's popular or safe. You *were* made to stand out in a way that reflects God's creativity and truth.

Think about it—Jesus didn't blend in. He didn't try to match what everyone expected. He lived fully as who God called Him to be, and it changed everything.

Stop hiding what makes you different. Start using it. The same qualities you think make you "weird" might be exactly what God wants to use to make a difference.

God's story needs what only ***you*** can bring. God made ***you*** to stand out—not for attention, but for a purpose that reflects Him. Stop trying to rewrite a story God already authored with love. ***You*** weren't made to match. **You were made to reflect.**

Growing up, being different often feels like being wrong. Different clothes? Lame. Different interests? Weird. Different personality?

"Try harder." It's like there's this invisible rulebook for what's "normal," and if you don't match it, you're out.

But here's the truth: that rulebook is trash. Because in God's view, different doesn't mean broken. It means **designed**. It means **set apart**. It means **equipped**.

When you spend your energy hiding what makes you different, you don't disappear. You just shrink into someone you were never supposed to be. But owning your differences? That's where real confidence begins. Not by becoming what you wish you were, but by **embracing** who you already are.

"Your hands shaped me and made me." — Job 10:8. God didn't copy-paste your life. He didn't mass-produce you or use a template. He **handcrafted** every part of you—your personality, your strengths, even your struggles. Not just the parts you're proud of, but the ones you're still trying to understand.

You weren't built for comparison. *You were built for purpose.* You're not ordinary. You're not a mistake. You are wonderfully made.

"He will take great delight in you; in his love he will no longer rebuke you, but will rejoice over you with singing." — Zephaniah 3:17. Think about that. God doesn't just put up with you—He delights in you. He sings over you. Not when you finally get it together. Not when you match everyone else. But right now. **As you are.**

He sees it all—your voice, your quirks, your strengths and weaknesses—and still calls you valuable. Not because you've earned it, but because you belong to Him.

"For we are God's masterpiece. He has created us anew in Christ Jesus, so we can do the good things He planned for us long ago." — Ephesians 2:10. You were created with beauty, value, and intention. Even the things that make you different are part of that design. God didn't just make you on purpose—He made you **for** a purpose.

So, what does it actually look like to live this out? Start by noticing what makes you unique. What do your friends come to you for? What lights you up inside? Maybe you're the guy everyone trusts to listen. Maybe you can make anyone laugh when things get tense. Maybe you see details others miss or create things that blow people away. That's not random—that's your God-given wiring in action.

Now think about the stuff you've been insecure about—the things you've been teased for or tried to hide. Here's the challenge: flip it. What made you feel "too much" might be exactly what someone else needs. Loud? You're wired to lead. Quiet? You see what others overlook. Always asking questions? You're naturally curious, which is how leaders are made.

Finally, walk it out. Pick just one trait and live it boldly this week. If you're funny, send a joke to a friend who needs cheering up. If you write, share a story or jot down a prayer for someone. If you build, help a neighbor fix something or start a project. If you notice people who feel left out, invite them to sit with you.

This isn't about proving yourself. It's about **showing up** as who you already are—and reminding the world it's okay to be real.

Let me tell you about a guy named Jordan. Jordan was the only one in his class who loved astronomy. While other guys talked about football, sneakers, or video games, Jordan talked about constellations and Mars rovers. He didn't do it to stand out—he just loved space.

At the school science night, he brought his telescope. He set it up, aimed it at the moon, and printed star charts to hand out. He was excited—maybe even proud. But most kids walked past without stopping. Some laughed. One kid joked loud enough for everyone to hear: "Who brings a space cannon to school night?"

Jordan laughed it off, but it stung. He almost didn't sign up for the next one. Maybe he'd switch to a "normal" topic—something safe and invisible. Blending in felt easier.

But something in him whispered: "Show up anyway." So, he did.

That night, something different happened. One kid quietly walked up and said, "Hey... that was awesome last time. Can you show me how to use it?" Jordan was surprised. This time, when he smiled, it was real. He didn't become the most popular kid. No party. No spotlight.

But something important shifted. Jordan realized he didn't need everyone to understand him. He just needed to stop hiding. Because his *willingness* to be different gave someone else permission to be curious too. Sometimes **standing out** is exactly what someone else needs to see.

Being different isn't a flaw. It's not something you need to fix or apologize for. Being different is how people find **hope**. It's how they see **courage**. It's how they realize they're not alone.

You don't need a crowd to prove you belong. You don't have to be loud to make an impact. Sometimes the bravest thing you can do is show up as ***yourself***.

So keep showing up—even when it feels awkward, even when no one else gets it, even when you're the only one. Someone out there might be waiting for your kind of different. And they won't see it unless you go first. Go first. Be brave. Someone's watching—and your courage might be the reason they stop hiding too.

Even when no one claps. Even when your voice shakes. Even when you feel like the odd one out—your difference still matters. And not just for you, but for someone else who's quietly watching, *hoping it's okay to be different too.*

So, start small. Show up once. Then again. And again. You don't need to announce it or prove anything. *You just need to walk in truth—the truth that your difference isn't something to hide. It's something to carry with* ***confidence****.*

That means the quiet way you think before you speak? That's *wisdom*. The energy you bring into the room? That's a *gift*. The way you always see things a little differently? That's *vision*.

It's not random. It's not weird. It's woven in for a reason.

You weren't made to chase the spotlight—but to reflect a bigger light. One that shines not because you're popular or perfect, but *because you're willing to live true to who God made you to be.*

So, what do you actually do when you feel like you're just too different? When comparison starts creeping in and you wish you could just blend in for a bit?

Start here:

Recognize the lie. That feeling of "not enough" is not the truth. That voice that says you have to be louder, cooler, more athletic, more normal—it's not from God. The enemy wants to shrink you with shame. God wants to free you with truth.

Name the truth. Say it out loud, write it on your mirror, whisper it in your prayer: God made me on purpose. He didn't mess up. My difference is part of the design. When you speak truth, you break the power of the lie.

Walk it out in one small way. Let your difference show up in the hallway. In the text you send. In the choice you make to sit with someone alone. You don't need a stage. You just need a step.

Here are a few things you can try this week to put that truth into action:

- **Write Down Three Things That Make You *You*:** Be specific—your sense of humor, your love for solving problems, your creativity, your loyalty. Remind yourself why those things matter.

- **Take a Brave Step with Your Strength:** If you're a builder, start that project. If you're a writer, finish that story. If you're a thinker, ask the deep question everyone else is avoiding. Don't wait for a crowd—just do the next right thing.

- **Celebrate Someone Else's Difference:** Look around. Who's standing out? Who's being brave just by being themselves? Tell them. You never know how much one word of encouragement can mean.

- **Thank God for the Way He Made You:** Take a few quiet minutes and actually thank God—not just for the good days or your talents, but for the ways He made you unique. The things you've wanted to hide? Thank Him for those too.

You'll still have days when it feels easier to go quiet. When someone makes a joke that stings. When fitting in feels safer than standing out.

That's okay.

But now? You know better. You know those differences were never flaws—they're **fingerprints**. *Evidence that you're a masterpiece, not a copy.*

You're learning to carry your difference with confidence. To walk in truth. To reflect the One who made you. And little by little, you're becoming the kind of person who helps other people do the same.

And that? That's impact.

So, the next time you feel like you don't fit in—look in the mirror. Look yourself in the eye. And remind yourself: I wasn't made to fit in. I was made to reflect Him. Your differences are real. But here's something worth knowing: even the guys who seem to have it all together? They're carrying something too.

Real Talk Mantra: ***You weren't made to fit in. You were made to reflect Him.***

Chapter Three

Everyone's Faking It (Even the Confident Ones)

Real confidence doesn't come from acting strong—it comes from being real.

You ever see someone walk in like they own the room? Head up. Confident smile. Like nothing could touch them? Everyone laughs at their jokes, calls out their name, daps them up like they're some kind of legend. The teachers like them. Coaches trust them. Girls notice them. Even the little kids want to be like them. And you sit there thinking, **Dang... must be nice to live like that.**

I used to think guys like that didn't struggle. That maybe some people just had this confidence thing figured out. Like they were born knowing what to say, how to move, what to wear, how to win. I figured there were two kinds of people—those who had "it," and those who had to fake it. And I was definitely in the second group.

But then something happened that flipped that idea upside down.

One afternoon after practice, I was hanging back to grab my water bottle. Everyone else had already cleared out except one guy and our coach. This dude was that guy—the one everyone liked. Loud laugh. Quick wit. Star player. MVP energy. But as I passed by, I caught part of their conversation. His voice wasn't booming like usual—it was quiet. Low. A little shaky.

He was asking if he was even good enough to stay on the team.

I froze.

Not because I was eavesdropping. But because I couldn't believe what I was hearing. Him? Doubting himself? The guy who seemed like he could bench press the school building and still have time to win class president? He was questioning if he belonged?

That moment broke something open in me. Suddenly confidence wasn't about swagger. It was about something hidden. Something nobody takes about.

Because suddenly it wasn't about swagger anymore. It wasn't about who laughs the loudest or walks the boldest. It was about something deeper. Something hidden.

It made me realize that most of the time, what we see on the outside isn't the whole story. In fact, a lot of people—especially the ones who look the most confident—are just really good at hiding their fear.

And we all do it. Maybe not the same way, but for the same reason.

We're scared someone will see through the act.

So, we start performing. And the longer we do it, the harder it becomes to remember what was real to begin with.

Maybe your performance is acting like you don't care. You walk through the hall like none of it matters. Grades? Whatever. Friend drama? Doesn't bother you. That invite you didn't get? Nah, you weren't trying to go anyway. **But inside? It stings. You care.** *You just don't want anyone to know.*

Or maybe your performance is doing everything right. You check every box. Say the right things. Win the awards. Stay busy. Stay productive. Because deep down, you're terrified that if you ever stopped performing, *you'd be forgotten.*

Or maybe it's jokes. You're the funny guy. The one who always has a comeback. You make everyone laugh. You keep it light. Because keeping it light means nobody will dig deeper. *Nobody will see the stuff you don't want them to find.*

All of these things—they're masks.

Not the kind you wear at Halloween or to stay healthy during flu season. I'm talking about invisible masks. The ones we slip on when we want to feel safe. The ones we wear when we think the real us isn't enough.

Here's what makes masks dangerous: at first, they feel like protection. They keep us from being embarrassed, from being judged, from standing out in the wrong way. But over time? *They start to shape us.* We wear them so often that we start believing the mask is actually who we are.

That's how the distortion works.

You stop being real and start being what you think people want. That's what the world is full of—people pretending, performing, and adjusting themselves just enough to fit in. And social media? It turns that pressure up to ten.

You scroll and see highlight reels—perfect moments, big wins, people with flawless skin, amazing lives, and captions that sound deep but don't say much. You start thinking, *They've got it all together. I'm the only one struggling.* But you're not.

That insecurity you feel—that doubt and the urge to keep pretending—it's not just you. It's all of us. Everyone's faking it sometimes, even the confident ones. Even the loudest ones. Even the people you look up to. And the longer we pretend, the heavier the mask gets.

God's not asking you to keep up the act. He's not clapping for your performance or impressed by your ability to look okay when you're falling apart. He sees through the image, the pose, the mask—and get this—He still chooses you.

That thing you're trying to hide, the weakness you hope nobody sees, the fear you wrestle with when the lights go off at night—God sees all of it. And He stays.

"Man looks at the outward appearance, but the Lord looks at the heart." — 1 Samuel 16:7.

People judge the surface. They see your confidence, your clothes, your status, your smile. But God sees past all of that. **He sees the part of you you don't show anyone**. And He doesn't flinch. He doesn't walk away. He doesn't say, "Come back when you've figured it out." He leans in.

Because real strength isn't about putting on a show. It's about being honest—especially with the One who already knows everything about you.

"My grace is sufficient for you, for my power is made perfect in weakness." — 2 Corinthians 12:9.

Perfect in weakness—not in pretending you're perfect, not in always acting confident. God's power shows up best when you stop faking it and start getting real.

"Come to me, all who are weary and burdened, and I will give you rest." — Matthew 11:28.

You don't have to keep holding it together just so people think you're strong. You don't have to perform to be accepted. He's not asking you to hide the mess—He's asking you to bring it to Him and breathe.

That's where **confidence** begins—not in being loud, but in being known.

It's where Micah's story begins too.

Micah was one of those guys who made life look effortless.

He wasn't just popular—he was magnetic. Charismatic. Always on. Everyone knew his name. He crushed class president speeches like he'd been born on a debate stage. He played guitar in the youth band, posted funny videos that actually went viral, and somehow made friends wherever he went.

You looked at Micah and thought, **If I had his life, I'd never struggle with confidence again.** But what nobody knew—what Micah never told anyone—*was that his confidence was cracking, fast.*

After every speech, he replayed his words in his head, picking them apart and convincing himself he sounded weird. After leading worship, he'd lie awake with his chest tight, feeling like a fraud.

He smiled constantly, but it was starting to feel like a costume. He was tired—worn thin from holding it all together—yet he kept the mask on. In his mind, if people saw the cracks, they'd stop trusting him. If he wasn't the strong one, the funny one, the "together" one... then who was he?

Then one night at youth group, something shifted. It wasn't the worship or the message that changed things—it was a question.

During small group, the leader asked everyone:

"What's one thing you've been pretending isn't a big deal—but it actually is?"

Micah felt his stomach twist. The room went quiet. But the silence didn't feel threatening. It felt... safe. No one was rushing him. No one was watching him too closely. It was just a pause, waiting for someone to go first.

Micah didn't even plan to speak, but then the words came out, soft and shaky: **"I'm tired of pretending."** Just four words.

He braced for awkward—expecting someone to laugh or make a joke—but instead, something happened that shocked him. His leader gave a slow, quiet nod, and another guy whispered, **"Me too."**

Micah didn't cry or give a big speech, but inside something broke free. For the first time in a long time, he wasn't hiding—and nothing fell apart. In fact, something better started to come together.

People didn't lose respect for him; they leaned in and listened more closely. He didn't lose his influence—he gained deeper connection. He didn't look weaker—he looked real, and that made him more trustworthy than ever.

Micah learned something most people miss: you don't get real confidence by faking it better. You get it by getting honest.

Here's what I wish someone had told me sooner: **Being honest takes more guts than faking it ever will.**

You don't need to be the loudest, smoothest, most put-together guy in the room to earn people's respect. What people actually respect? Honesty. Vulnerability. The courage to say, **"I don't have it all figured out, but I'm trying."**

You think people are looking for perfection—but they're actually just hoping someone else will go first. Someone who's real. Someone who admits they're struggling and doesn't flinch when it gets uncomfortable.

And yeah, not everyone will get it. Some people might make dumb comments or not know how to respond. But a lot more people? *They'll feel relief. Because you going **first** gives them permission to breathe, too.*

You don't have to show everything to everyone. But find at least one safe person—someone who's for you—and let them see behind the mask. Because hiding might feel safer at first, but honesty always builds deeper strength in the long run.

And remember this: you don't have to fake it with God.

There's no mask convincing enough to hide what's going on inside you from Him. And that's a good thing. Because the very parts you're afraid to show are the places *He wants to meet you with grace.*

God doesn't call you to "man up" and muscle through it alone.

He invites you to lay the weight down.

Confidence that's built on *pretending* will eventually **crack**.

Confidence that's built on *truth*? That's what holds **steady**—no matter who's watching.

Here are a few things you can try this week to start living with real confidence:

- **Write down one thing you're afraid to admit—and tell God about it.** Whisper it in prayer. Or jot it in a journal. Let it out. That's where healing starts.

- **Send a short text that encourages someone else.** A simple *"Hey—I'm proud of you"* or *"You're doing great"* reminds you that your words have power too.

- **Take a 24-hour break from social media.** Notice how quiet your mind gets without the comparison noise. More peace, less pressure.

- **Give someone a compliment based on character, not looks or popularity.** Try something like, *"You're always really thoughtful,"* or *"I admire how hard you work."* Seeing value in others helps you notice it in yourself too.

- **Do one brave thing this week.** Speak up in class. Admit when something's bothering you. Try the thing you've been scared to fail at. Then reflect on how it felt. Bravery doesn't mean you weren't scared—it means you didn't let fear win.

You'll still have moments when you feel like throwing the mask back on. That's okay. Old habits don't break instantly. But now you know there's a better way—and you've taken the first step.

You're not chasing some fake version of strength anymore. You're learning to live real. Honest. Unedited.

And that? **That's where confidence is born.**

Even on the days you still feel unsure, remember this: God isn't waiting for the polished version of you. He **already** loves the real one.

The one who gets overwhelmed sometimes. The one who doubts. The one who's trying.

Take off the mask. Let someone see you and let God lead you.

Because you don't have to pretend to be strong anymore.

You're already stronger than you think. So, if everyone's faking it, and the mirror lies, what's actually true? That's exactly where we are going next.

Real Talk Mantra: ***You don't have to fake strength to be confident. Real confidence comes from being real.***

Chapter Four

What Does God Actually Think About Me?

Moving past self-doubt to hear the truth God already speaks.

You can grow up in church, know all the songs, memorize the verses, and still lie awake at night wondering what God actually thinks about you. I know, because I've been there.

I knew when to raise my hands during worship and when to bow my head during prayer. I could win the verse memorization games, say all the right things in youth group, and even smile politely when someone said, "God loves you." But behind all of it was a question I couldn't shake loose.

Does God really love me like that?

Not just when I'm singing. Not just when I'm behaving. Not just when I'm doing everything right.

But when I mess up for the fifth time in a week? When I'm zoned out during prayer? When I forget to read my Bible or lose my temper again? Does He **still** choose me?

I wanted to believe He did. I'd heard it enough times that it should've stuck. *"God loves you no matter what."* But it felt like something you'd slap on a bumper sticker—a nice idea, not the kind of truth that could hold you up when your shame starts shouting louder than your faith.

And maybe no one said it out loud, but the message I picked up was this: **God loves the good version of me.** The cleaned-up one. The faithful one. The one who tries hard. But the messy version? The inconsistent one? The one who's struggling to even feel spiritual at all? That version, I was sure, disappointed Him.

It didn't matter that I knew the Bible verses. I still imagined God with His arms crossed, sighing in frustration every time I slipped. I figured His grace had a limit, and I was testing it weekly.

When the lights went out at night and I was finally alone with my thoughts, I wasn't praying bold, confident prayers. I was quietly wondering if maybe... **God had already started giving up on me.**

That's the lie that sneaks in quietly but lands hard: **God's love has limits.** He's for me when I'm strong, but distant when I'm weak. Close when I'm worshiping, but far when I'm stumbling. Maybe not angry—but tired. Disappointed. Done.

When you believe that lie long enough, your faith starts to shrink. It turns into a performance, a habit, a list of things to do so God won't leave.

So you keep showing up—singing the songs, saying the prayers, hoping it's enough to prove you're serious. You try to be better. You try to "fix" whatever's broken inside you.

But it still doesn't feel like enough.

Because underneath it all is the fear: **What if I've messed up too much?** What if God doesn't want someone like me anymore?

If you've ever asked those questions, I need you to know something: **God is not pacing in frustration, waiting for you to finally get it right.** He's not disappointed that you're struggling. He's not tired of hearing from you. He's not looking for the perfect version of you before He calls you close. **He already sees you—the real you—and He's not backing away.**

When you can't see that clearly, the silence fills with fear. You start imagining what God might be thinking. You assume the worst. You brace for rejection. You try to clean up your act, hoping maybe then, maybe, He'll look your way again.

That's the distortion. It's not that God has changed—it's that **our vision has.** Shame fogs up the mirror. Guilt warps what's true. And pretty soon, you're not hearing God's voice anymore. You're just hearing echoes of your own insecurity.

And that's why this question matters so much: **What does God actually think about me?**

Not the version I perform. Not the image I try to maintain. But the actual me. The me who wonders. The me who fails. The me who's trying... but still not sure I'm enough.

Because if you never answer that question with the truth, the lies will fill in the silence every time.

You don't have to guess what God thinks about you. **He already told you.**

When the lies start creeping in—*I'm not good enough... I'm a disappointment... I've probably gone too far this time*—you've got to fight back with something stronger than your feelings. You need something unshakable. Something that won't change just because you had a bad day.

That's where God's Word steps in.

"See what great love the Father has lavished on us, that we should be called children of God! And that is what we are!" — 1 John 3:1

Not distant followers. Not tolerated mistakes. **Children.** God doesn't hand out love like grades—He gives it like a Father who's already claimed you. He doesn't say, *"Try harder and maybe I'll love you."* He says, *"You're already Mine."*

Even when you zone out during prayer. Even when you're battling doubt. Even when shame tries to tell you otherwise.

"The Lord is close to the brokenhearted and saves those who are crushed in spirit." — Psalm 34:18.

God isn't looking for perfect faith. **He draws near when your heart is heavy.** That means you don't have to fake spiritual strength to be close to Him. You don't have to pretend everything's fine. God moves toward brokenness. He meets you in it.

"I have loved you with an everlasting love; I have drawn you with unfailing kindness." — Jeremiah 31:3.

Not a love that shifts with your mood. Not a kindness that runs out when you fail. **Everlasting. Unfailing.** That means His love doesn't hit pause when you mess up. It doesn't fade out when you forget to pray. It's steady—strong enough to hold you, even when you don't feel like you're holding onto Him.

"Therefore, there is now no condemnation for those who are in Christ Jesus." — Romans 8:1.

You are not being followed around by a scorecard. **God's not waiting to read off your list of failures.** There is no trapdoor under your faith. No courtroom where you're about to be found guilty. If you belong to Jesus, your sin doesn't define you—**grace does.**

That's where Noah found himself.

He came to youth group most weeks, but you wouldn't know it by looking at him. Hoodie up. Earbuds in. Sat in the back and mostly kept his head down. He wasn't disrespectful, just... distant. Like he didn't really expect anything there to be for him.

Noah believed in God. He just didn't believe **God believed much in him**. He thought faith was for the polished kids—the ones who knew the worship songs, shared their testimonies, and cried during altar calls. He felt like an outsider looking in. Not because anyone pushed him out, but because he had already **disqualified himself** in his own mind.

Then one Wednesday night, something unexpected happened. The leader handed out blank index cards with one question:

"What do you think God sees when He looks at you?"

Noah stared at the card. His mind filled with flaws: *lazy, distracted, failure.* Someone who should be better by now. Someone who probably disappoints God. He didn't even want to write it down.

But then the leader read a verse:

"For we are God's masterpiece, created in Christ Jesus to do good works, which God prepared in advance for us to do." — Ephesians 2:10

One word stopped Noah cold: **masterpiece.**

He didn't feel like a masterpiece. He felt like a mess. But that word—it wouldn't leave him alone. **What if God sees more than I do?** Not just the past. Not just the mess. But the *masterpiece* in progress.

So, he wrote it, slowly: *God doesn't just see my mess. He sees His masterpiece in progress.*

He folded the card and tucked it in his hoodie pocket. That night, back home, he looked in the mirror and taped the card to the corner. Not because he suddenly felt worthy or because everything changed, but because maybe... he was starting to believe what God had already said.

You don't have to **feel** like a masterpiece to **be** one.

That's one of the hardest and most freeing things to accept. Real faith isn't about always feeling it—it's about choosing to believe what God says is true, even when your emotions haven't caught up yet.

Some days you'll wake up and believe it easily. Other days you'll stare into the mirror and only see the mess. But on every kind of day, this truth stays the same: **God sees the real you—and He still calls you His.**

Not *"His project."* Not *"His regret."* **His child. His masterpiece. His.**

The enemy will try to mess with your identity. That's always been the move—confuse how you see yourself, so you forget what God has already declared over you. If he can keep you tangled in doubt, stuck in shame, distracted by fear, then he knows you'll stop living like someone who's deeply loved.

But that ends when you stop letting shame be your script.

Start asking a better question: **Do the voices in my head actually sound like God's voice?**

His voice doesn't sound like shame. His voice may challenge you, but it won't crush you. It brings **conviction, not condemnation.** Growth, not guilt trips. Truth, not threats.

The more you learn what He really sounds like, the easier it becomes to call out the lies when they show up.

You don't have to earn your way back into His presence—you're already welcome there. You don't have to clean up your thoughts to be accepted—He already sees them. And still, **He draws near.**

You pause the noise—and reset the truth:

- **Tape *Ephesians 2:10* to your mirror**. Read it when you're brushing your teeth. Whisper it when your thoughts start spiraling. *You are God's masterpiece, created on purpose, for a purpose.* Not perfect. But chosen.

- **Change your lock screen to a verse that reminds you who you are**. One sentence of truth can interrupt a flood of lies. Keep it in front of you. Let it reshape how you see your reflection.

- **Say it out loud when doubt creeps in:** *God, help me see myself the way You do.* It doesn't have to be long or fancy—just honest. Every time you say it, you're pushing back the dark.

- **When you're brave enough—share it**. Tell a friend or mentor one thing you believe God sees in you. Speaking truth makes it real, and when someone else hears you say it, they might just believe it for themselves too.

This isn't about pretending to be confident. It's about learning to see what God sees—**slowly, consistently, honestly.** And choosing to believe it again tomorrow if you have to.

You're not behind. You're not disqualified. You're not forgotten.

You are becoming. And what God starts, He doesn't abandon.

So, when the lies get loud again—and they will—don't argue with them in your head. Go straight to the Source. Pull out His Word. Remind yourself of what's real. Say it out loud if you have to. Stick it to your mirror, your heart, your thoughts.

Because **God's love isn't just a concept. It's a constant.**

You are not a mistake. You are not invisible. You are not too far gone.

You are loved. Deeply. Steadily. Always.

So even if you still feel messy, even if the doubts aren't all gone, even if you're only beginning to see what He sees—hold on.

God already sees the masterpiece in progress. And He's not walking away. Now you know what God thinks about you. The harder question is what to do when everything inside you feels like it's going sideways and you don't have words for why.

Real Talk Mantra: ***God sees the real me, calls me His masterpiece, and He's not walking away.***

Part 1 Recap: Who Am I, Really?

Seeing Yourself Clearly

You've made it through the first part of this journey. You've stared into the mirror and started clearing away the lies that once felt louder than the truth. You've seen that different isn't broken — it's part of God's intentional design. You've learned that confidence isn't about faking it; it's about being real with what's going on inside.

And you've started asking the most important question: *What does God actually think about me?*

Here's what we've learned together:

- **The mirror doesn't define you — God does.**
- **You weren't made to blend in — you were made to reflect Him.**
- **You don't have to fake confidence to belong — real confidence comes from being real.**
- **God sees the real you, calls you His masterpiece, and He's not walking away.**

Maybe you're beginning to believe this is true about you. And even if it still feels messy, that's okay. You don't have to have it all figured out. You're not behind. You're becoming who God made you to be — step by step.

Pause & Reflect:

- What's one truth you'll carry forward from this part — and why?
- What lie started to lose its grip on you?
- What's one thing you did differently that made you feel more like the real you?

Next Up: Life's Hard, and That's Normal

You've started to see who you really are. Now we're stepping into the harder stuff — the moments that make you feel stuck, small, or too far gone.

But here's the truth: **You're not stuck. You're not alone. You're not too far gone. God's already in it with you.** And we'll walk through it — together.

Part 2: Life's Hard, and That's Normal

Exploring emotions, mistakes, and real life—with honesty and hope.

Let's be honest—this stage of life can feel like a rollercoaster you didn't exactly sign up for. One minute, everything clicks. You crush a test, make your friends laugh, hit the shot, and think maybe you've finally found your rhythm. The next day, something small knocks you off course—a harsh comment, a missed assignment, a weird silence in the hallway—and suddenly, everything feels heavy.

Your chest feels tight. You're irritated for no reason. You zone out, scroll too long, or get mad at people who didn't do anything wrong. And you start to wonder, *Is it just me? Shouldn't I be handling this better by now?*

If you've ever asked that, hear me: you're not broken. You're not weak. You're human. And more normal than you think.

This part of the book is about the stuff guys usually don't talk about—not because it's not real, but because we've been trained to keep it in. We'll talk about emotions that feel too big to carry. About the moments after you mess up and the guilt won't let go. About family and friendships that feel complicated. About the times you feel completely alone—even in a crowd.

We're going to name the things most guys shove down and pretend aren't there. Not to make them bigger—but to walk through them with truth.

And here's the good news: you don't have to walk through any of it alone. God's already with you. Not from a distance. Not waiting for you to "get it together." Right here. Right now. In the middle of the mess, the questions, and even the silence.

You don't need to fake strength. You don't need perfect answers. You just need to be honest.

Because this part of your story—the confusing, hard, not-yet-figured-out part—it matters. And how you face it will shape who you become.

So let's face it—together.

Chapter Five

The Anger, the Shame, and the Ugly Cry

Real strength isn't pretending you're fine. It's being honest enough to feel.

Sometimes it's not one big thing that breaks you. It's a thousand small things stacked so high you can't breathe. You keep brushing them off—*It's fine. I'm fine. It's no big deal.* Until it is.

You know the kind of day I'm talking about. Nothing dramatic happens. No giant explosion. Just one thing after another, like bricks on your chest. An annoying group project. A dumb comment. Someone looking at you sideways. A grade that doesn't match your effort. You tell yourself to suck it up. Be chill. Move on. But then something tiny tips the scale—and suddenly it all comes crashing down.

That's what happened to Alex.

He didn't get into a fight. He didn't have a major breakdown at school. He just carried more than he let on. His group project partner slacked off, and he picked up the slack. Then they got a C, and his partner laughed it off like it didn't matter. Alex clenched his jaw and nodded like it was cool. It wasn't.

He carried it home like a backpack full of bricks. Pretended he was good. Put on the smile. Played it chill. But when his little brother asked for the last Pop-Tart, something snapped. Cabinet slammed. Voice raised. *"No! You always get everything!"* And just like that—tears. Not the quiet, single-drop kind. Full-on ugly cry. Shaking. Snot. Couldn't speak.

It didn't make sense. Not at first. It wasn't about the Pop-Tart. It wasn't even just the project. It was everything he'd stuffed down. All the pressure. All the emotion. All the things he didn't know how to say out loud. And it finally broke free.

That's how it works. *Emotions don't disappear when you ignore them.* They collect. They press. They wait. And eventually, *they find their own way out.*

Most of us guys don't really know what to do with that. We're not taught how to feel. We're taught how *not* to feel. Keep it together. Be tough. Don't cry. Don't talk about it. Shake it off. Keep moving.

Maybe nobody told you that directly, but the message was there. Coaches. Classmates. Maybe even people at home. If you felt pain, you buried it. If something hurt, you brushed it off. If something scared you, you kept it quiet. Because being emotional was seen as weak. And *weak wasn't allowed*.

So you smile when you're hurt. You laugh when you want to yell. You bottle it all up so you don't make anyone uncomfortable. And you learn to act like nothing's wrong even when you're falling apart.

For a while, it kind of works. You survive. You keep moving. You even convince yourself you're okay.

Until one day, a Pop-Tart sets it all off.

And you're standing there, overwhelmed and embarrassed, wondering where it even came from.

But here's what no one tells you: *feeling your emotions doesn't make you weak.* ***Ignoring*** *them does.*

If you burn your hand and feel nothing, that's not strength—that's danger. Pain isn't the problem. It's the signal. It's what tells you, *Hey, something's wrong. Pay attention.*

Same with emotions. They're not random. They're not the enemy. They're signals. Messages. Warnings. Clues. And if you keep shutting them down, eventually you lose the ability to read them at all.

That's when numbness shows up. And numb doesn't mean strong. It just means you've stopped letting yourself be honest.

And God never asked you to live numb.

He gave you emotions for a reason. They help you process pain. They connect you with people. They push you toward truth. They were never meant to be buried—they were meant to be brought to Him.

But somewhere along the way, we believed a lie: *Real guys don't cry. Real guys don't feel. Real guys suck it up and deal.*

And that lie? It's left a lot of us walking around angry, anxious, or exhausted—with no clue how to fix it. Because we were never given permission to feel what we're feeling. Just instructions to hide it better.

That's not strength. *That's survival.* And God has something way **better** than survival for you.

Jesus didn't hide His emotions—and He's the Son of God.

When His friend Lazarus died, Jesus didn't just say *"God's got a plan"* and move on. He stood there with people who were grieving and wept. Not a tear trickling down His cheek—He broke down in front of others. No shame. No apology. Just honest sorrow.

"Jesus wept." —John 11:35.

The Bible doesn't call emotions a problem. It gives us a way to bring them to God. There's a reason the book of Psalms is filled with everything from celebration to rage to heartbreak. David didn't just sing about victories—he screamed about betrayal, cried in caves, begged for help, and told God exactly how lost he felt. **And God still called him a man after His own heart.**

"Cast all your anxiety on Him because He cares for you." — 1 Peter 5:7.

Not some. Not just the parts that sound "churchy." *All.* That means your fear, your shame, your stress, your silent breakdowns in your room at night—God cares. You don't have to pray fancy words. Just be real. God isn't scared of your emotion. He's already seen it. And He stays.

"The Lord is close to the brokenhearted and saves those who are crushed in spirit." — Psalm 34:18.

That word *"close"* means God doesn't walk away when you're a mess. He leans in. When you feel like you're too much—too emotional, too overwhelmed, too lost—He doesn't back off. He moves closer.

Isaiah knew what it was like to keep everything bottled up.

He was the kid everyone counted on. Teachers loved him. Coaches trusted him. Parents bragged about him. Good grades. Respectful attitude. Solid athlete. If there was a model student poster, Isaiah would've been on it. People said he had it all together.

What they didn't see was how much pressure that put on him.

Isaiah wasn't faking it—he really did care. He wanted to do well. He wanted to be helpful. But after a while, it stopped feeling like a gift and started feeling like a trap. Being *"the good kid"* meant never messing up, never saying no, never showing weakness.

So he stuffed it.

And one day, it cracked.

At basketball practice, the coach yelled across the court, *"Isaiah! Hustle! You're barely trying!"* It wasn't even that harsh. But the moment it hit, something inside Isaiah folded. His face flushed. His legs moved, but his mind just shut down. He muttered, "Sorry," and jogged to the bench like nothing happened.

But everything had.

That night, he didn't say a word to anyone. He walked into his room, shut the door, grabbed his pillow, and screamed into it until his throat hurt and his tears soaked the cotton. He wasn't just mad at the coach. He was mad at everything.

Mad that being dependable made him feel invisible. Mad that everyone noticed his effort but no one noticed his exhaustion. Mad that he felt like a robot instead of a person.

He didn't know how to tell anyone. So he didn't. *But the tears? They told the truth.* They were his body's way of saying what his voice hadn't learned how to say yet: *I'm not okay.*

Here's the truth no one tells you when you're trying to be strong: silence doesn't heal anything.

You can bottle it, bury it, pretend it's not there—but eventually it shows up somewhere. In your attitude. In your anger. In your anxiety. And maybe you don't even know why it hits you so hard. But underneath it all, it's the weight you've been carrying without anyone noticing.

You weren't made to carry all of that alone.

Real strength isn't pushing past your feelings. It's being brave enough to name them. To sit with them. To let God hold them with you instead of trying to power through like a machine.

You weren't made to be numb. You were made to be honest.

When emotions stack up, don't wait for the meltdown. Don't wait for the slammed door or the yelling match or the moment when you scare yourself with how out of control it feels. Start small. Let honesty become your first response—not your last resort.

Take a breath and whisper, *"God, I can't hold this anymore. Help me calm down. Help me see what's true."*

Then name it. Not just "I'm mad" or "I'm fine." Get underneath it. *I feel invisible. I feel rejected. I feel like I always mess things up. I feel like nobody cares.* Let the emotion be specific. That's where the healing starts.

Trace it back. Ask yourself where it's coming from. Was it something that happened today? Or something that's been building for weeks? Is it one moment—or the weight of too many?

And then talk to God. Out loud if you can. Or write it. *God, I'm overwhelmed. I don't know how to fix this. I don't even know what I need. I just know I need You.*

God doesn't need perfect words—He just wants the real ones.

He's not tired of you. He's not shaking His head. He's not backing away because you feel too much. He's staying.

And after you talk to Him, do something to release the weight. Move your body. Go outside. Stretch. Shoot hoops. Journal. Cry. Breathe. Call someone who gets it. Emotions aren't just spiritual—they're physical. They need space to move through you.

One small shift can make a big difference:

Each day this week, **tell God one honest feeling**—even if it's just a word. Whisper it while brushing your teeth. Say it while you walk to class. Let it become normal to bring your heart to Him.

Write it down. Keep a simple note on your phone or in a journal. You don't need full sentences—just scraps of truth. A place to let pressure out before it explodes.

Move. Not for attention. Not to fix anything. Just to let your body help you reset. It could be a walk, a jog, or tossing a ball in the yard. Movement releases what you don't always have words for.

Memorize truth. Keep Psalm 34:18 or 1 Peter 5:7 somewhere close. Let those words be your anchor on the days emotions feel too big to name.

And when you're ready—**tell someone.** One trusted person. A friend, mentor, coach, or leader. Say one honest sentence. That's all it takes to open the door to support.

You don't have to cry in front of a crowd. You don't have to give a speech. Just take one honest step out of hiding.

God is closer than you think. He sees the breakdown before it happens. He hears the words you can't form. He knows the reasons behind the rage, the silence, the fake smile.

And still, He stays.

You don't have to fix it all today. But you can start by not stuffing it anymore.

Let the tears come. Let the anger be prayed instead of buried. Let the sadness find its way into the light. None of it makes you weak. It just makes you human. And fully seen by a God who doesn't walk away.

You don't have to hide how you feel to be strong. You just have to be honest with the One who already knows. Naming what you feel is the first step. But what do you do the days when you don't just feel bad? When you actually did something wrong?

Real Talk Mantra: ***I don't have to hide how I feel to be strong. God sees the real me—and He stays.***

Chapter Six

I Messed Up. Now What?

God's grace is bigger than your guilt—and it's never too late to start again.

You know that feeling when your stomach drops and your brain starts screaming, *Oh no, I can't believe I just did that*? Yeah. That was me—on full display—in front of my entire science class.

It was supposed to be my redemption moment. I'd actually prepared this time—really prepared. My slides were lined up. My notes were memorized. I even had a dumb joke ready, one I'd rehearsed in the bathroom mirror the night before, just to lighten the mood and prove to myself I could be confident up there.

I walked to the front, trying to look calm even though my palms were slick with sweat. The clicker felt heavier than it should have. My heartbeat was so loud I could almost hear it in my ears. I clicked the first slide and—blank. Total mental whiteout.

It was like my brain shut the lights off and locked the door. My hands trembled so badly I had to grip the podium just to keep them still. My throat locked up. The carefully rehearsed opening line? Gone. The dumb joke? Vanished. Even the bullet points I'd stared at a hundred times looked like a foreign language.

A few kids glanced away with that awkward *I don't want to watch this train wreck* kind of look. Then it happened—one short chuckle from the back. Not loud, but it might as well have been on a microphone. That tiny laugh hit harder than any insult.

When I glanced at my teacher's face, I couldn't tell if it was sympathy or disappointment—and somehow, not knowing made it worse.

The joke I'd planned? Never left my lips. Instead, I muttered something about "technical issues," fumbled to the end slide, and took my seat. It was the longest forty seconds of my life.

No one said anything afterward. But they didn't have to. I had already done the damage myself: *You blew it. You looked dumb. Everyone's going to remember this forever.*

That night, lying in bed, I didn't replay the parts that went okay. I didn't think about how I'd at least shown up and tried. I replayed the failure. Over. And over. And over. Until it wasn't just, *I messed up that one time.* It was, *I'm the guy who fails.*

If you've ever been stuck in a moment like that, you know how heavy it feels. And it's not always a presentation. Sometimes it's missing the game-winning shot. Sometimes it's a joke you wish you could take back. Sometimes it's the silence—something you should have said but didn't.

Either way, that gut-punch arrives. That voice whispers, *You let everyone down. You let yourself down.*

That's guilt. And guilt is sharp. It's heavy. It sneaks into your thoughts when you're brushing your teeth or trying to fall asleep.

But here's something most people never say out loud: guilt isn't always the enemy. Sometimes it's a gift.

Think of it like the pain you feel when you touch something hot. That sting is your body's way of saying, *Pull your hand back before you get burned worse.* Guilt can be like that—God's way of saying, *Hey, something's off here. Let's fix it.*

The real enemy? **That's shame.** They're cousins, but they're not the same thing. Guilt says, *I did something wrong.* Shame says, *There's something wrong with me.*

And here's the dangerous thing about shame—it's sticky. Guilt is like a smoke alarm: it's loud and annoying, but once you deal with the problem, it turns off. Shame is like a song stuck in your head, replaying on loop until you start to believe it.

Shame says, *You always mess up. You'll never be enough. Why even try?*

One time when I was younger, I forgot my baseball cleats on game day. I had to play in old, flat sneakers with no grip. I slipped going for a ball in the second inning, missed an easy play, and I could hear the reaction from the stands. We finished the game, but that sound stayed with me. I heard it in my head the rest of the week. It didn't stay, I made an error. It turned into, I'm the guy who lets the team down.

That's what shame does—it turns a single moment into your identity.

And that voice? That's never God's. God doesn't rub your face in your mistakes. He doesn't throw them back at you years later. He doesn't stand with His arms crossed, waiting for you to "earn" your way back. He meets you right there—knee-deep in the mess—not to label you, but to lift you out.

You can mess up and still be **loved.** Still be **seen.** Still be **chosen.** Still be **used by God.**

So what do you do when you've blown it? When the words are out, the damage is done, and you wish you could rewind the day?

You start with this: own it. Say the words out loud: *I messed up.* Not *I messed up, but...* followed by an excuse. Not *I messed up because they...* and shifting the blame. **Just own it**. Because it's not weakness to admit the truth—it's the first step to being free from it.

Then you take it to God. Not with the "right" words or the perfect churchy prayer. Just honesty. He already knows what happened. He's not surprised or shaking His head in disgust. He's leaning in, listening, ready to forgive, restore, and help you heal.

If there's a way to make things right—do it. Apologize. Send the text. Walk up to them in the hallway. Even if your voice shakes, even if they don't respond the way you hope, it matters. Owning what's yours to own is how growth begins.

Here's what's incredible about God's grace: you're going to mess up again. That's part of being human. But every single time, His grace is still part of your story.

"If we confess our sins, He is faithful and just and will forgive us our sins and purify us from all unrighteousness." — 1 John 1:9.

You might feel like your mistake is now your name tag—like forever you'll be "the one who blew it." But God says otherwise:

"Therefore, if anyone is in Christ, the new creation has come: The old has gone, the new is here!" — 2 Corinthians 5:17.

You're not just patched up. You're **brand new.** Even on the days you still feel broken. Even when you're still figuring it out.

God whispers, *"My grace is sufficient for you, for my power is made perfect in weakness." — 2 Corinthians 12:9.*

He doesn't wait for you to finally be strong enough to deserve His help. He meets you in the guilt, in the shame, in the mess—and that's exactly where He works best.

I once saw this truth come alive in a guy named Caleb.

Caleb was the funny one in his group—the guy who could get the whole table laughing. Most of the time, his humor was harmless. But one day at lunch, without thinking, he made a joke about a friend's dad who had just lost his job.

The moment the words hit the air, the whole atmosphere shifted. The laughter stopped. His friend's eyes dropped to the table. Caleb felt the punch of regret instantly.

That night, the replay loop ran in his mind over and over—not just what he said, but the way his friend's face fell. He thought about walking past him the next day, but something in him said, *Don't hide from this.*

So he stopped, no jokes this time. Just four simple words: "I'm really sorry, man."

It didn't erase what happened. It didn't instantly make everything okay. But it was a start. And sometimes a start is exactly what God can use to turn something around.

You're going to mess up. We all do. You'll say things you wish you could take back. You'll cross lines you never meant to cross. But one mistake—one moment—doesn't erase who you are or the story God is still writing.

The question isn't *if* you'll mess up. It's *what you'll do next.*

Owning it takes courage. Apologizing takes strength. Learning from it? That's growth.

When you choose to be honest instead of hiding, that's when grace steps in. And grace has this crazy way of taking the thing that made you feel disqualified... and turning it into the very thing God uses to help someone else later.

Rebuilding after a mess-up isn't about pretending it never happened—it's about taking small, honest steps forward. Here are a few to try this week:

- **Write It Out:** Open your notes app or grab a notebook. Write a short, honest prayer: *"God, here's where I blew it... and here's where I need You."* Don't dress it up. Don't edit it. Just get it out of your head and onto paper.

- **Send Some Encouragement:** Even if things feel awkward with someone, send a quick message: *"I've been thinking about you. I've got your back."* It reminds them you care and reminds you that you still have purpose.

- **Memorize Truth:** Write 1 John 1:9 somewhere you'll see it this week: *"If we confess our sins, He is faithful and just and will forgive us..."* Let it interrupt your guilt spiral with the promise of grace.

- **Say "I messed up":** If you've been avoiding an apology, find the words and say them. Owning the mistake breaks its grip on you.

- **Do the Next Right Thing:** You don't need a 30-day plan to move forward. Just take one step today that reflects who you want to be, not the mistake you made.

Here's the truth—*you are not your mistake*. You're not the awkward science presentation. You're not the missed shot, the bad joke, or the moment you froze. You're not "that kid who failed" or "the one who always gets it wrong." That's not your name.

Your name, in God's eyes, has never changed: **chosen**, **loved**, **forgiven**. And nothing you've done—not your worst day, not your biggest regret—has the power to rewrite that.

God's grace is not fragile. It doesn't get weaker with every mistake you make. It's steady. Stubborn. Unshakable. It will meet you in the middle of the hallway when you're terrified to make eye contact. It will walk into the locker room when you'd rather hide in the corner. It will sit with you in the quiet moments when no one else is around and whisper, *You are still Mine.*

You've learned how to handle messing up. Now comes something harder: handling the people who mess with you.

Real Talk Mantra: ***God's grace is bigger than my guilt—and it's never too late to start again.***

Chapter Seven

People Are Hard (But Worth It)

Why the people closest to you sometimes make life the hardest—and how to respond without losing yourself.

It was just a regular Tuesday. School, homework, the usual background noise of life. But sometimes the background noise turns into something else.

The voices in the kitchen weren't loud, but there was a sharpness in them that made my chest tighten. I paused in the hallway. My parents were at it again—not shouting, but in that clipped, cold tone that somehow feels worse because it's controlled. Words like knives, careful but still cutting.

I stepped into the kitchen, hoping to stay invisible. Just rinse my plate, get out. But before I could, my mom made a comment about the dishes piling up—her voice like a tap turned too far to the hot side. My dad sighed—not angry, just tired. But somehow, the sigh made me feel like I was the problem, even though I hadn't done anything.

I mumbled something, set my plate down harder than I meant to, and headed for my room. The door closed with a dull thud—not a slam, but enough to let my frustration out. I turned on music, not because it was my favorite song, but because it was louder than the storm in my head.

Then my phone lit up. For a second, I thought maybe it was my best friend finally texting back. But no—it was just a group chat. I scrolled up and saw my last three messages to them. Unanswered. Or maybe just one-word replies that used to be full conversations. I stared at the bubbles, replaying the last thing I said. Did I do something wrong? The silence felt heavier than the noise from the kitchen.

You can be surrounded by people and still feel completely alone.

And here's where the distortion creeps in—the lie that maybe you're the problem. That if you were easier to be around, people wouldn't pull away. That if you were better—funnier, smarter, more likable—things would go back to normal.

But it's not just you. You're not too much. You're not the only one who feels this way. The truth is—**people are hard**. Even the ones we love. Especially the ones we love.

Every person you meet is carrying ***something***—stress, insecurity, fear, wounds you can't see. And when what they're carrying collides with what you're carrying, it can feel like a constant tug-of-war between staying close and protecting yourself.

School makes it even messier. One minute you're laughing with friends, the next you're wondering if you're still part of the group. One day your parents are proud of you, the next you feel like you can't do anything right. It's disorienting. Exhausting.

So what do you do when your "people" don't feel safe anymore? When the distance, the tension, or the silence starts to build? Most of us want to either explode or disappear.

But there's another way—**honesty**.

Honesty isn't unloading everything you've ever felt or trying to win an argument. It's naming what's really going on before it grows into something uglier. Saying, "I feel left out." Or, "I don't know what I did, but something feels different." Asking, "Are we okay?" instead of assuming the worst.

The Bible gives us anchors for moments like this—truth you can grab onto when relationships feel like they're drifting or sinking.

"If it is possible, as far as it depends on you, live at peace with everyone." — Romans 12:18.

That little phrase *"as far as it depends on you"* is huge. It's God's way of reminding you that peace isn't about controlling the other person—*it's about **controlling** what's in your hands.* You can't force the group chat to respond. You can't change the tone in the kitchen. You can't guarantee someone will hear your side or agree with it.

But you can choose *your* part. You can keep your words respectful even when theirs aren't. You can take a breath instead of firing back. You can decide to build a bridge—even if the other person doesn't meet you halfway.

Peace isn't always possible. But **doing your part always is**. And when you're doing your part, the next verse shows you exactly how to keep your cool when emotions start boiling over.

"Everyone should be quick to listen, slow to speak and slow to become angry." — James 1:19.

This is the opposite of how most of us naturally react when we're hurt. Usually, we're quick to speak, quick to post, quick to clap back—and even quicker to get angry. But God flips that script.

Quick to listen means you actually give the other person space to explain, even if you're convinced you're right. *Slow to speak* means you pause long enough to make sure your words help instead of hurt. *Slow to become angry* means you give God space to calm your heart before you decide how to respond.

It's not weakness—it's **wisdom**. That pause is where God steps in. That pause can save a friendship, keep peace at home, *or at least protect your heart from spiraling into bitterness.* And if you're wondering what love is supposed to look like in those tense moments, the next verse paints the picture.

"A friend loves at all times, and a brother is born for a time of adversity." — Proverbs 17:17.

Loves at all times doesn't mean a friend never gets frustrated with you. It means they don't vanish when things get hard. They keep showing up—when you're stressed, when you're not at your best, when the conversation feels awkward.

And *born for a time of adversity* means that real friends, and real family, are there when life gets messy—not just when it's easy. The truth is, not everyone in your life will be this kind of person. **But you can choose to be one**.

You can choose to be steady when someone else is falling apart. You can choose to lean in instead of pulling away. You can choose to love the way God loves you—*faithful, patient, present.*

Jaden learned this the hard way. One night, his little sister accidentally broke his gaming headset. She didn't mean to—but that didn't matter in the moment. Jaden saw the cracked plastic, and something in him snapped.

His voice came out sharp. Too sharp. He yelled. Slammed his door. Called her "stupid." The word hit harder than he realized—it landed on her face like a slap. Her eyes filled with tears, and she ran to her room without a word.

His parents came in frustrated—partly about the yelling, partly because they knew this wasn't just about the headset. "You need to calm down," they told him. But Jaden wasn't calm. His heart was still racing, his chest tight.

When the adrenaline wore off, he just sat on his bed, staring at the wall. The anger started to drain, and in its place came a heavy, ugly feeling—regret.

That's when it hit him: it wasn't really about the headset. It was the bad grade earlier that day. The missed homework he didn't want to explain. The awkward lunch where no one saved him a seat. The group chat silence that made him feel invisible all week. The headset was just the spark that lit a whole pile of frustration he'd been carrying.

The next morning, Jaden made a choice a lot of people—especially teens—never make. He went to his sister's room, knocked softly, and said, “I’m sorry.” Not in that quick, mumbled way that gets it over with, but in a way that made her look up and see he meant it.

“I shouldn’t have called you that. I was mad, but that wasn’t okay.” Her eyes softened. “It’s okay,” she said quietly. And in that moment, the air between them shifted.

Then he found his parents in the kitchen and told them the truth—not as an excuse, but as a confession. “I’ve been stressed, and I took it out on her. I shouldn’t have done that.”

Did it magically fix everything? No. His headset was still broken. His grade was still low. The group chat still hadn’t lit up with his name. But something had changed—because he had.

It cost him his pride. And that was exactly the point.

He’d chosen humility over pride. Honesty over hiding.

We all have “headset moments.” Times when one little thing—someone’s tone, a forgotten invite, a sarcastic comment—pushes us over the edge, but the truth is, the reaction isn’t about that one thing. **It’s about *everything else* we’ve been carrying.**

When that happens, you have two choices:

- **Double down** and let your pride keep you in the wrong.
- **Step up** and own it, even if the other person isn’t perfect either.

Here’s the hard truth: you can’t control how they respond, but you *can* control whether you make the first move toward repair.

Apologies aren't weakness. They're a strength most people avoid because they cost something—your ego. But every time you choose humility, you break the cycle of hurt. You open the door for God to bring peace where there was tension.

And just like Jaden, you might find that owning your part—no matter how small—does more to restore a relationship than waiting for the other person to "deserve" your kindness.

Rebuilding or protecting a relationship doesn't mean you have to fix everything in one conversation. Sometimes it's about taking **one small, honest step** and letting God grow something from there.

Try these this week:

- **Start the conversation:** Send a simple message to someone you've been distant from: "Hey, can we talk soon?"
- **Cool down before reacting:** If something hits you wrong, give yourself ten minutes. Step outside. Pray for calm.
- **Notice the good:** Say one kind thing to someone close to you, even if things have been tense.
- **Ask instead of assuming:** "Are we okay?" is better than silent guessing.
- **Pray for them—even if you're upset:** Prayer doesn't just change them—it changes **you**.

People will let you down. And you'll let them down too. But every time you choose love instead of bitterness, every time you try again instead of shutting down, you grow into someone stronger, someone more grounded, someone more like the one God is shaping you to be.

Maybe today, your "people" feel distant, sharp, or impossible to reach. Maybe your best friend is leaving you on read. Maybe your parents are distracted and quick to criticize. Or maybe you're the one who said or did something that built a wall.

You don't have to solve it all by tonight. But you can choose one step. One text. One kind word. One pause before reacting.

Because when you choose to show up instead of shutting down, you aren't just protecting the relationship—***you're protecting your heart from growing hard.***

God never said relationships would be smooth sailing. But He promised His love would be steady enough to carry you through the waves. His grace isn't just for forgiving your mistakes—it's for strengthening you to love others when it's hard.

So, take a breath. Step back into the kitchen, the group chat, or the conversation you've been avoiding. Not because you know exactly how it will turn out, but because **God's grace is enough to meet you in the middle of the mess**. People are hard. And sometimes the loneliest moments don't happen when you're by yourself. They happen when you're surrounded by people who don't really see you.

Real Talk Mantra: ***People are hard—but God gives me grace to love anyway.***

Chapter Eight

When You Feel Alone (Even in a Crowd)

You're not invisible. God notices you—even when no one else does.

It was lunchtime, and the cafeteria was packed. **Laughter** bounced off the walls, trays clattered, voices overlapped like waves crashing on a shore. It was loud, chaotic, alive.

But me? I felt like a **ghost**. Like I wasn't even there. Right in the middle of all that noise, I felt completely *unseen.*

I sat with friends—or at least, people who used to feel like friends. They were talking, laughing, sharing **inside jokes** I didn't understand. I tried to join in. I told a joke. I made a comment. Nobody looked up. Nobody responded. Someone laughed, but not at what I said.

I stared at my tray, poked at my food, and told myself it didn't matter. **But it did.**

There was this **weight** in my chest—like sadness and rejection mixed together. And that's when it hit me: *the loneliest place isn't always your bedroom late at night.* Sometimes, it's a **crowded room** where everyone sees your face, but **nobody really sees you.**

Loneliness is tricky. It doesn't always look like sitting by yourself. You can be surrounded by people—in class, at practice, even at home—and still feel like you're on an **island** no one notices.

You laugh at the right times. You say the usual things. You act like you're part of the moment, but inside, you feel **disconnected**. Like you're watching life happen from the outside.

Sometimes it shows up at night when your phone stays quiet and no one reaches out. Sometimes it hits while scrolling through **highlight reels** online—smiles, group selfies, birthday shoutouts—and your name isn't there. Sometimes it creeps in slowly, like **fog** you didn't notice until everything feels gray.

And you start asking hard questions: *Is it me? Why am I always the one left out? Do I even matter?* Those thoughts swirl and spiral until you want to disappear or pretend to be someone else just to feel noticed.

But you're not broken for feeling this way. You're **human.** And almost everyone—at some point—has sat in a room full of people and wondered if anyone truly saw them.

Sometimes the disconnect isn't even your choice. Maybe your best friend moved away. Maybe the group changed and you didn't get invited. Maybe your family feels distant even when everyone's in the same room.

Or maybe nothing obvious happened—you just woke up one day and felt **left behind.** That doesn't make you weak. It doesn't mean something's wrong with you. It means you're **human.**

But here's the truth you need to hold on to: *feeling alone doesn't mean you are alone.* And it definitely doesn't mean you're stuck here forever.

I know what it feels like to think nobody notices—not even God. You start to believe He's distant, like everyone else. But that's **not** the truth.

God sees every part of you—especially the parts you think nobody notices.

He sees the version of you that **smiles** even when you're tired, the you who **quietly shows up** while feeling like nobody would miss you if you didn't.

He notices the moments when you scroll through your phone, wondering if anyone will reach out, and the late nights when you lie awake replaying conversations you wish had gone differently.

He hears the thoughts you don't say out loud—all of them—and **He never looks away.**

"Even if my father and mother abandon me, the Lord will hold me close." — Psalm 27:10.

People might let you down, even the ones who promised they'd be there. Friends get busy. Families get distracted. Sometimes people you trust drift away without explaining why.

But **God doesn't walk out.** He steps closer when everyone else steps back, moving toward you not out of obligation but out of **love.**

"I am with you always, even to the end of the age." — Matthew 28:20.

Not sometimes. Not only on good days. **Always.**

When your heart feels heavy—when the loneliness gets loud—**He is still there.** When you feel forgotten, His presence is proof you are not.

And when the ache becomes too much—when it feels like your chest can't hold one more sigh—the Bible reminds you:

"The Lord is close to the brokenhearted and saves those who are crushed in spirit." — Psalm 34:18.

If you feel crushed or unseen, you are exactly where God moves closest. You don't have to fake a smile for Him or clean yourself up to earn His attention. You don't have to "get over it" before you talk to Him—**He's already there** in the silence, in the tears, and in the moments, you think no one could possibly understand.

You are **fully seen.** You are **fully loved.** And you are never truly alone.

That was something Miles understood all too well.

Miles wasn't the loud kid in the room. He didn't jump into every conversation or toss out jokes that made everyone crack up. But he had his small circle—two or three close friends who made the day feel lighter.

For a while, that was enough.

Then one of them moved away.

At first, Miles thought things wouldn't really change. The group still hung out, still texted, still met up at lunch. But the **energy** was different. Conversations moved faster. Inside jokes—ones he didn't know—started flying. He'd smile like he got it, but inside, he didn't.

Group texts turned into one-word replies. Lunch at their usual table felt quieter—not because the cafeteria had changed, but because Miles wasn't part of the **rhythm** anymore.

And the thought crept in: *Would anyone even notice if I stopped showing up?*

So, he tried it.

The next youth group night, he walked in late. He didn't weave through the crowd to sit with his usual people—he slipped into the back row, half-hidden by a column. No one called his name. No one waved him over. After the last song, he grabbed his jacket and left before anyone could catch him.

At school, he took his lunch to the **library.** At first, he told himself it was to finish homework. But if he was honest? It hurt less than sitting at a table where he felt **invisible.**

It's strange how you can be surrounded by people and still feel like nobody in the room actually knows you're there.

For a couple of weeks, Miles ran the same experiment—pull back just enough to see if anyone would notice. And the results felt like confirmation of his worst fears. Nobody said anything. Nobody asked where he was. And each time that happened, the voice in his head got louder: *See? You don't really matter to them.*

That's the distortion loneliness creates—it makes you believe **silence equals worthlessness.** That if people don't say anything, it must mean you don't matter. But the truth? People can care and still miss the signs. Their quiet isn't proof of your invisibility—it's proof they're human.

Miles didn't actually want to disappear. He wanted someone to prove he didn't have to.

One Wednesday night at youth group, the pastor's topic was **loneliness.** Miles wasn't expecting much—he had already decided to just sit through the talk and head out like usual. But somewhere between the Bible verses and the personal stories, the pastor said something that stopped him cold:

"Sometimes God's answer to loneliness starts with you letting one person in."

Miles sat there, heart pounding. His first instinct? Leave. It would be easier to avoid the risk, to slip out before anyone could see through him. But something in him stayed planted in that seat.

When the service ended, he didn't bolt for the door. He waited—until the noise in the room dropped, until most people had filtered out. Then he walked up to one of the leaders, his voice barely above a whisper: *"I think I've been feeling really alone lately... can you pray with me?"*

That moment didn't fix everything. But it **cracked something open.**

The leader prayed with him right there—and remembered him. The next week, Miles got a text: *"Hey, you coming tonight?"* The week after that, he was asked to help set up chairs. Later, to help clean up.

It was slow. Sometimes awkward. There were still nights when he felt like maybe he didn't belong. But week by week, the quiet wall around him started to **loosen.** Not because he suddenly had a hundred new friends, but because one person saw him—and kept seeing him.

Looking back, Miles realized something: while he was waiting for people to notice him, **God had been noticing him the whole time.** God had been guiding him toward that one conversation, that one leader, that one open door.

When everyone else seemed to pull away, the Lord held him close. When he felt abandoned, God was still saying, *"I am with you always."* When the loneliness spiked, God didn't just watch from a distance—He stayed in it with him and helped him take one small step at a time.

That's the thing about **God's presence**—it doesn't just comfort you in the loneliness. Sometimes, it leads you out of it.

So, if you're feeling invisible right now, don't wait for the perfect group to magically appear. Take one small step. Say one honest sentence. Look for the one person who feels safe enough to hear it.

Yeah, it feels risky. Yeah, there's a chance someone won't respond the way you hoped. But there's also the chance that your **honesty** opens the door for real connection. And that's worth the risk.

Here are some simple steps you can try this week:

- **Send a low-pressure text.** Just say, "Hey, how's it going?" or "Haven't seen you in a while—want to hang out?" You're not asking for a deep heart-to-heart—you're just opening the door.

- **Show up once.** Pick one thing you've been avoiding—youth group, lunch with that one friend, practice—and go. You don't have to stay long or be the life of the party. Just show up.

- **Ask instead of assuming.** If someone feels distant, say, "Are we okay?" instead of letting the silence grow.

- **Speak life into someone.** Say one kind thing to a person you've been distant from. A genuine compliment can soften walls on both sides.

- **Sit with God in the quiet.** No phone, no distractions—just a few minutes reading Psalm 27 or Psalm 34 and asking Him to show you where He's already close.

You don't have to solve loneliness in one leap. You don't need a perfect friend group overnight.

All it takes is one small, honest step. Then another. Each one is like a crack in a dark wall—letting in just enough light to remind you the darkness isn't forever.

Even when no one else notices, **God notices.**

Even when you feel unseen, **He's holding you close**—not waiting outside the door of your loneliness but *sitting in it with you until the walls come down.*

And even when loneliness feels louder than hope, **His presence is louder** still reminding you that you are loved, wanted, and worth pursuing.

So, take the step. Send the text. Stay the extra five minutes. Whisper the prayer. Let His voice be the loudest in the room.

You are not forgotten. This is not the end of your story. You are seen. You are not alone. Now it's time to talk about what it actually means to become.

Real Talk Mantra: ***I am seen by God, loved as I am, and never truly alone. One honest step is enough to begin again.***

Part 2 Recap: Life's Hard, and That's Normal

The Hard Stuff

You've made it through the second part of this journey. You've faced the feelings, the mistakes, the messy relationships, and the quiet ache of loneliness. And you've learned something huge—**none of it disqualifies you from becoming the guy God made you to be.**

Here's what we've seen together:

- Feeling deeply doesn't make you weak—it's where healing begins when you let God meet you in it.
- Messing up doesn't define you—grace is always bigger than guilt.
- People are complicated, but honest steps and God's wisdom can bring peace and restore connection.
- Loneliness doesn't mean you're forgotten—you're fully seen and never truly alone.

And maybe—just maybe—you're starting to believe that even in the hardest moments, God hasn't walked away. He's been here the whole time, shaping you through every struggle.

Pause & Reflect:

- When was one time in this part where you saw God show up in your mess?
- What truth from these chapters do you want to carry forward when life feels heavy again?
- What's one step you can take this week to let God meet you in the hard stuff instead of handling it alone?

Next Up: Becoming the Guy God Made You to Be

You've seen that life is messy—and that's normal. But you're not stuck. Now **it's time to step forward into who God designed you to be—with courage, strength, and faith** that's real in the everyday.

Part 3: Becoming the Guy God Made You to Be

Living with Character, Courage, and Real Faith

You've looked in the mirror. You've faced the hard stuff. And now—you're ready for the next step. This is where who you *are* turns into how you *live*. Not just on good days, not just when life is easy, and not just when people are watching—but in every moment, especially the ones no one else sees.

Because **who you are when no one's looking—that's who you really are**. And who you're becoming in the small, quiet, everyday choices—that's what lasts.

This part of the journey is about character that holds steady, even when it costs you. About courage that stands up, even when fear tries to shut you down. About faith that's not just for Sundays, but one that walks with you through the hallway, the locker room, the bedroom, and even the battle in your own mind.

We're not chasing hype here. We're chasing truth. And the more you lean into that truth, the more it shapes you into someone stronger, wiser, more grounded—and more like Jesus.

So take a deep breath. We're stepping forward—together.

Chapter Nine

What Makes a Man (Hint: It's Not Muscles)

Strength is more than size—it starts in your character.

In school, gym class was more than just a time to play games or run laps. For a lot of us, it felt like a silent test—a measuring stick for who was *"man enough"*.

The second you stepped into that echoing room, it was like the rules changed. The squeak of sneakers on the polished floor, the sharp whistle of the coach, the smell of rubber balls and faint sweat—it all seemed to whisper, *Let's see what you're made of.*

If you were one of the tall guys, the fast guys, or the ones who already had biceps you liked to show off, you didn't have much to worry about. You got picked first for dodgeball, laughed the loudest during stretches, and carried this invisible badge of toughness.

But if you were still growing into your body—maybe slower, smaller, or just not as confident—it felt completely different. Every drill felt like a spotlight was on you, and you weren't sure you wanted to be seen.

I remember one particular day like it was yesterday. Coach lined us up for pushups. *"We're going for twenty,"* he barked, pacing like a drill sergeant.

The first kid dropped to the floor and cranked them out like it was nothing. Everyone around him nodded, impressed. Then the next guy. And the next.

By the time it got to me, my stomach was in knots. I lowered myself down, arms trembling almost instantly. By pushup number two, my elbows wobbled.

I could hear sneakers squeaking nearby, a couple of snickers behind me. I tried to block them out, but it was like they got louder with every shaky movement. My arms burned. My face got hot. I glanced at the floor, pretending to fix my hand placement, hoping no one noticed that I just couldn't keep going.

And somewhere in the middle of that short, humiliating set, a question sank in: *Is this what it means to be a man?* Muscles? Toughness? Being the guy who can keep going when everyone else stops?

The thing is, I didn't just leave that thought in the gym. It followed me into the locker room, where the "strong" guys made harmless-seeming jokes that still stung. It followed me into the hallways, where the ones who could run the fastest or jump the highest seemed to hold some kind of unspoken rank.

And it followed me home, where I stared at my reflection and tried to figure out if I had what it took to measure up.

For a long time, I believed that **strength** was something you could see. That being a man was about impressing people—about proving yourself in ways that could be counted or measured. And honestly? I was exhausted from trying.

What I didn't know yet was that the **strongest people** I'd ever meet wouldn't be the loudest, the tallest, or the ones with the most muscle. They'd be the ones who **quietly chose to do the right thing** when it would've been easier not to.

We live in a world that throws a lot of pressure at young guys like you. Be tough. Don't cry. Always win. Never show weakness. And if you do feel something? Bury it. Smile like you're fine. Keep moving.

It's subtle sometimes, but it's everywhere.

A coach who tells you to *"walk it off"* when you're hurt, even if you can barely stand.

A dad or uncle who jokes, *"Man up,"* when something actually scares you.

A friend group where everyone's roasting each other but no one's actually talking about what's real.

Social media clips of guys with six-packs, perfect hair, and fast cars—sending the message that you've got to look a certain way, own certain things, or hit certain achievements before you matter.

For a lot of guys, manhood becomes a performance—a role you play. You throw on this invisible armor every morning, telling yourself, *I can't let anyone see the cracks.*

You learn how to hide the soft parts of you because somewhere along the way, someone convinced you that being gentle, scared, or sad was the same thing as being weak.

But here's the truth: that kind of pressure doesn't build real men. **It builds masks.** And masks can feel safe… for a while. They can protect you from teasing, from judgment, from the risk of opening up. But they also keep you from being truly known.

And God never called you to live hidden. He didn't design you to live your whole life acting tough but feeling alone inside.

God's version of **strength** isn't about pretending you're bulletproof. It's about **standing when everything in you wants to sit down**. It's about **staying kind when someone snaps at you**. It's about **owning your mistakes** when you'd rather shift the blame. It's about **forgiving** even when no one else would expect you to.

That kind of strength rarely trends online. No one's making TikToks about the guy who takes out the trash without being asked, or the kid who admits he was wrong and apologizes. But **heaven notices**. And God calls it powerful.

Look at the way Jesus lived. The strongest man who ever walked the earth didn't prove His strength by crushing His enemies or building His image. He showed it by washing His disciples' dirty feet. By staying silent when false accusations flew. By forgiving the very people who nailed Him to a cross. By choosing to lay down His life when He could've walked away in an instant.

If you want to know what kind of **strength** God values, it's right there in His Word. *"Be strong and courageous. Do not be afraid; do not be discouraged, for the Lord your God will be with you wherever you go"* — Joshua 1:9.

Strength doesn't mean you never feel fear. It means you choose to move forward *with God* even when you do. Think about that—God's telling you He will be **with you wherever you go**. Not just in the locker room when you're confident, but in the moments you want to disappear. Not just when you win, but when you lose and feel like you've got nothing to offer.

"I, the Lord, search the heart and examine the mind, to reward each person according to their conduct, according to what their deeds deserve" — Jeremiah 17:10.

God's not handing out trophies for who can lift the most weight or who has the best highlight reel. He's looking at the *heart*. He's looking at how you treat people when there's nothing in it for you. He sees the times you tell the truth even when lying would be easier. He notices when you include the person everyone else ignores. Those things may not trend online—but they matter in heaven.

"My flesh and my heart may fail, but God is the strength of my heart and my portion forever" — Psalm 73:26.

Even the strongest guy you know will eventually have a bad day, a weak moment, or a failure that knocks him down. You will too. And that's okay—because God's strength doesn't fade. When you've got nothing left, when you're tired of holding it all together, His strength can carry you. You just have to let Him.

The world will always tell you to build muscles. **God tells you to build character.**

Brandon wasn't the most popular guy in school. He wasn't the kind to fight for the spotlight or be the loudest in the room. He was the kind of guy who noticed things—small details other people missed.

There was a kid in his school named Mason. Mason always seemed to move through the hallways like he was hoping no one would see him. His hood was up more often than not. He sat in the back row, spoke so quietly you had to lean in to hear him, and wore the same couple of shirts on repeat.

People noticed—but not in the kind way. They whispered about him. Laughed when he tripped. Made jokes that weren't really jokes.

One rainy Tuesday morning, Brandon was standing near the front doors when Mason walked in. Just as he stepped onto the tile, one of his backpack straps snapped. The bag hit the ground, the zipper broke open, and everything spilled out—books, loose papers, a crumpled lunch bag. A science project—a cardboard volcano—rolled across the floor into a puddle of rainwater.

For a moment, everything froze. Mason bent down fast, trying to grab his stuff, his shoulders curling in like he wanted to disappear. A few kids laughed. One pulled out a phone to record. Most just stepped around him.

Brandon felt his chest tighten. *This is awkward. Don't make it worse. Just keep walking.*

But then another thought hit him—*If I don't help, who will?*

He unzipped his backpack and pulled out a crumpled grocery sack from the bottom. Crouching beside Mason, he held it open. "Here—let's get it out of the water before it's ruined," Brandon said quietly.

Mason's eyes flicked up, surprised. He didn't say much—just nodded. Together, they picked up the soggy folders, the damp notebook, the volcano that now looked more like a lopsided hill. Brandon carried half the load and walked with Mason to the office to see if someone could help fix the strap.

There was no applause. No big *"hero moment."* Brandon just went to class after that, like nothing happened.

But something had happened.

For Mason, it was the first time in a long time that someone saw him—not to make fun of him, not to judge him, but to **help**. That one small moment chipped away at the wall he'd been building around himself.

For Brandon, it was the moment his definition of **strength** shifted. It wasn't about pushup counts or standing out in the crowd. It was about showing up when it counted—even if nobody else noticed.

And that's the thing: the kind of strength God values rarely trends online. It doesn't need a stage or a scoreboard. It just needs you to care enough to show up when nobody's watching.

So here's the question you've got to ask yourself: **What kind of strength are you building?** The kind that *gets likes*? Or the kind that **lasts**?

Because one day, the weight you can lift won't matter nearly as much as the people you **lifted when they were down**.

Every time you choose **character over cool**, you're becoming the kind of man God made you to be—not perfect, not flawless, but *real*.

And here's the best part—you don't have to wait until you're older to start. You can start now.

Here are a few ways to build the kind of strength that lasts:

- **Apologize without excuses.** *"I messed up—and I'm sorry"* carries more weight than pretending it never happened.
- **Help someone without being asked.** Even a small act says, *I see you.*
- **Encourage someone overlooked.** Your words might be the only kind thing they hear all week.
- **Walk away from drama.** Even if it costs you popularity, peace is worth more.
- **Speak what's real.** Choose honesty over hype, even if it's uncomfortable.

These aren't *small* things. They're **training**. Every time you do them, you're building the kind of **muscles that never fade**—the ones in your heart, your character, your faith.

You're not too young. You're not too late. And you're not too weak. God's already working in you, **strengthening you one choice at a time**.

So take a breath. Stand tall. Step forward, even if your voice shakes. That's what makes a man.

Knowing what real strength looks like is step one. Taking the first step when you're scared? That's where it gets real.

Real Talk Mantra: ***Real strength isn't loud—it's built in the quiet, honest choices that reflect God's heart.***

Chapter Ten

Doing Hard Things, Even When You're Scared

Real courage isn't the absence of fear. It's trusting God enough to take the next step anyway.

The climbing wall didn't look that bad from across the field. From a distance, it had the same vibe you'd see in a summer camp brochure—bright helmets, big smiles, maybe a quick group photo before everyone headed to the snack bar. It almost looked inviting.

But the closer Eli got, the more that "fun adventure" feeling started to fade. Up close, the wall didn't just look tall—it looked *massive.* It towered over him like a giant wooden skyscraper, each handhold suddenly smaller and farther apart than it had seemed a few minutes ago.

His stomach tightened. The harness around his waist felt too snug. The helmet strap pressed against his chin until it was hard to swallow. His hands—already clammy from the summer heat—slipped inside the too-big, borrowed gloves, the kind that smelled faintly like sweat from a hundred climbs before his.

This was supposed to be a "team-building challenge." That's what the youth pastor had said. *It's going to be awesome.* Eli wanted to believe him. He wanted to be the guy who laughed from the top, waving down at the group below. But right now, standing at the base, all he could think about was what would happen if he failed.

And not failed at the top. Failed from the *very first step.*

Someone from the group shouted, "You got this, Eli!" but the words floated past like paper in the wind. They didn't stick. They didn't make him feel "got." They just reminded him that everyone was watching.

His heart pounded so hard it felt like it might crack his ribs. The sound in his ears was so loud it drowned out everything else. The wall loomed above him, and the weight of the moment pressed on his shoulders—not just the height, but the unspoken dare. The fear of looking weak. The fear of trying and still not being enough.

Every part of him wanted to back out. To laugh it off. To say something like, "Nah, I'm good," and melt into the crowd. His mind screamed, *Don't do it.* His legs felt heavy, like they'd been filled with sand.

And then—underneath all that noise—another voice rose. Quieter. Steadier. It whispered, *Just take one step.*

So he did. Knees shaking. Palms sweating. One step up. Then another.

It wasn't fast. It wasn't pretty. There was no movie moment where he suddenly looked like a champion climber. But he kept moving. Not because the fear disappeared—it didn't—but because he decided to move *anyway.*

Later, when he was back on the ground, someone asked if it had been scary. Eli didn't shrug or pretend it was nothing. He just nodded and said, "Yeah. But I did it anyway."

Fear's like that.

It's loud. It moves into your chest, sits heavy in your stomach, and wraps itself around your thoughts. Sometimes it's the voice that says, *You're not good enough.* Sometimes it's the pressure that whispers, *If you fail, everyone will know.* It can make your throat tighten, your palms sweat, and your thoughts spin like a tornado you can't slow down.

But here's what most people miss—fear itself isn't what stops you. Fear is just noise. It's letting that noise decide what you do that actually holds you back.

You can be scared and still move forward. You can feel nervous and still take the step. The goal isn't to erase fear completely. The goal is to keep it from driving the car.

And courage? It's usually not what you expect.

It's not always running headfirst into danger with a battle cry. More often, it's quiet. Small. Easy to miss. It looks like showing up when you'd rather stay home. Like apologizing when your pride tells you to shut down. Like raising your hand even when your voice shakes.

Fear shows up everywhere—

- Trying out for the team, knowing you might not make it.
- Owning a mistake instead of covering it up.

- Praying out loud in a group for the first time.
- Admitting to someone, "I'm not okay."

Sometimes, the scariest steps are the ones no one else even notices.

And here's the part you can't forget—those moments when you feel weakest? They're often the best moments for God to show up. He's not standing at the top of the wall saying, *Come back when you're ready.* He's standing right next to you, saying, *I'm here now. Let's go.*

The world doesn't make it easy to face fear.

Everywhere you look, courage gets packaged like an action movie. Big explosions. Epic one-liners. The hero walks away without a scratch, cool music playing in the background. That's the version most people think they have to live up to.

And if you can't? Then maybe you're not "brave" enough.

It's a trap—this idea that courage only counts if it's loud, fearless, and Instagram-worthy.

The truth is, that's not real courage. That's performance. And performance has a dangerous side effect: if you don't *feel* like the hero in the movie, you start to believe you're not brave at all.

The lies creep in—

- **Lie #1:** *If I'm still scared, I must not have faith.*
- **Lie #2:** *If I can't do it perfectly, it's not worth trying.*
- **Lie #3:** *If no one notices, it doesn't matter.*

Those lies will keep you locked up. They'll keep you standing at the base of your own climbing wall—watching, waiting, convincing yourself you'll "try later" when you feel ready.

But here's the thing—*ready* is a myth. If you wait until the fear's gone, you might be waiting the rest of your life.

God never said courage means you'll stop feeling afraid. He said something better—**you don't have to face fear alone.**

In Isaiah 41:10, He says, *"Do not fear, for I am with you... I will strengthen you and help you; I will uphold you with my righteous right hand."* That's not a pep talk from far away—it's a promise from right beside you. He doesn't say, "Come back when you're braver." He says, "I'll go with you, step for step."

Psalm 56:3 puts it plainly: *"When I am afraid, I put my trust in you."* Notice it says *when*, not *if*. God already knows fear is going to show up in your life. But He's also telling you exactly what to do with it—put it in His hands and keep moving.

And 2 Timothy 1:7 drives it home: *"God has not given us a spirit of fear, but of power, love, and a sound mind."* That voice telling you you're not enough? That's not from Him. His voice says the opposite:

- **Power**—to take the step.
- **Love**—to know you're not alone.
- **A sound mind**—to stay steady when the noise in your head gets loud.

God doesn't measure courage by how confident you look—He measures it by whether you trust Him enough to act. Even if your hands are shaking. Even if your voice cracks. Even if your legs feel like they're made of concrete.

The people we read about in the Bible didn't wait until the fear was gone. Moses still doubted his words. Gideon still felt small. Esther still knew she could be killed. But every one of them moved anyway—*and that's where God met them.*

The same is true for you. Courage isn't about being fearless—it's about being faithful.

Liam had always been the "safe" kid. Not in a bad way—he followed the rules, stayed out of trouble, and didn't like doing anything that might make him look foolish. If there was even a small risk of embarrassment, he was out.

So when his history teacher announced that everyone in class would have to give a five-minute presentation *alone* in front of the whole class, Liam's stomach dropped. He could already feel the heat creeping up his neck. Speaking in front of people was his personal nightmare.

For a week, he found excuses not to start. He told himself he'd "prepare later." He thought about faking being sick. He even considered asking if he could turn in an essay instead. But every time he pictured standing up there, the same thought pressed in—*What if I mess up? What if everyone sees me crash and burn?*

The night before the presentation, Liam was pacing in his room when his older sister walked in. "You're wearing a path in the carpet," she teased. But when she saw his face, her smile faded. "You're scared, huh?"

Liam nodded.

She sat on his bed. "You don't have to do it perfectly. You just have to do it scared." Then she handed him a sticky note with Isaiah 41:10 scribbled on it: *Do not fear, for I am with you... I will strengthen you and help you.*

The next day, Liam stood behind his desk as the teacher called his name. His knees wobbled. His mouth was dry. His hands shook as he carried his notecards to the front. But the sticky note was in his pocket, and he could almost hear his sister's voice: *Do it scared.*

He stumbled over the first sentence. He forgot a line in the middle. But he kept going—one breath, one sentence, one slide at a time. And when it was over, he realized something: fear hadn't disappeared, but it hadn't stopped him either.

It wasn't a perfect presentation. But it was a win—because he'd moved forward anyway.

Here's the thing—**courage isn't a feeling you wait for. It's a choice you make** *while* you're still nervous, unsure, or shaking a little.

If you're waiting until you "feel ready," you'll be standing still for a long time. That's why God doesn't say, *When you're fearless, then I'll go with* you. He says, *I'm with you now—so move.*

I know what fear can do. It can make your chest tight and your brain spin with every worst-case scenario you can imagine. It convinces you that "safe" is better than "faithful." But the truth? **Safe doesn't**

grow you. And God is far more interested in growing you than keeping you comfortable.

If you want to start building courage right where you are, here are four things you can do today:

- **Call it out.** Don't just say "I'm scared." Name the exact fear. The more specific you are, the smaller it feels.
- **Trade the lie for the truth.** Ask, *What does God actually say about this?* Find a verse, a promise, or a past moment where He came through.
- **Take one step.** It can be tiny—send the text, speak up once, walk into the room. *You're not climbing the whole wall today, you're taking one handhold.*
- **Celebrate every try.** Every time you move while afraid, you're getting stronger. That's courage training.

When you live like that, fear stops being the boss. It doesn't disappear—but it loses the driver's seat. And in its place, something stronger takes over—**trust**.

You might not be facing a climbing wall. Maybe for you, it's trying out for the team. Owning a mistake. Praying out loud. Asking for help. Saying *I'm not okay*. Whatever it is, fear doesn't mean stop. It just means something matters.

And God? He's already in the moment you're afraid of. Already ahead of you. Already strengthening you. So instead of trying to feel fearless, try this: **trust Him enough to take the next step scared**.

Sometimes that next step might be so small it feels silly—like walking into the room you've been avoiding, hitting "send" on the text you've rewritten ten times, or raising your hand when you'd rather shrink back. But small doesn't mean unimportant. In God's hands, small steps have a way of changing your whole direction.

There will be days when you hesitate. Days when fear feels louder than faith. Days when you feel like you're climbing in slow motion while everyone else seems to be running ahead. On those days, remember—God isn't keeping score by your speed. He's looking at your trust. Every time you choose Him over the fear, **you're winning**.

Some of the bravest people you'll ever meet are carrying fear in one hand and faith in the other. They're just choosing to let faith lead. That's what makes them brave. And that's something you can choose too—right here, right now.

- **Name what scares you.** Write it down. Call it out. Let it stop living rent-free in your head.
- **Say it to someone safe.** Tell a friend, mentor, or God Himself. Fear shrinks when truth steps in.
- **Try one small thing.** Raise your hand. Speak up. Start. The motion matters more than the mastery.
- **Pick a verse and keep it close.** Isaiah 41:10 or Psalm 56:3 are great ones. Post it. Pray it. Preach it to your fear.
- **Encourage someone else.** Fear isolates. Bravery connects. Reach out to someone else who might be scared too.

You're going to have moments when fear punches first—hard. When everything in you wants to shrink, hide, or quit. But you don't have to be fearless to be brave. You just have to move with God, even when your voice cracks and your knees shake.

So, when fear says, *Don't try*, remember that's not God talking. He's saying, *Let's go. I'm with you.*

You were made for **brave things**. Not because you've got it all figured out—but because you belong to the One who does. Courage for the big moments matters. But what about the ordinary ones, the Tuesday afternoons nobody sees? That's where faith actually grows.

Real Talk Mantra: ***Courage isn't the absence of fear—it's trusting God enough to take the next step anyway.***

Chapter Eleven

Faith Isn't Just for Sundays

Bringing God into your everyday, not just your weekend.

But then Monday hits—and it's like you left God behind in the youth room.

You ever notice how easy it is to act *"spiritual"* at church? You know the drill—you sit in the right spot, say the right words, sing when everyone else is singing. Maybe you even raise a hand during worship if the moment feels right. You play the role, and no one questions it.

I used to be that guy. At church, I could quote verses and pray out loud like I'd been doing it my whole life. I smiled like everything was good, nodded when the leader talked, and played the part well enough that no one would think I was struggling. But when I walked into school the next day, it was like my faith had an *off switch*. I wasn't doing anything "bad," really. I just didn't bring God with me—into the locker room, into my conversations, into my late-night anxiety or those moments when life felt confusing and real.

It's almost like I thought faith was a weekend-only thing—a Sunday outfit you put on, wear for a few hours, and then hang back up until next week. At church, I could talk about God. But at lunch on Tuesday? In group projects? When I was scrolling at 1 a.m.? I acted like He wasn't there. The shift for me didn't happen in a church service. It happened on a Tuesday, sitting in my car in a school parking lot, whispering something so short it barely counted as a prayer. But it was the most honest thing I'd said to God in months.

And maybe you've been there too. Maybe your faith feels real when the lights are low and the music is loud, but it gets fuzzy in between. Or maybe you don't know how to connect with God outside of the church building. It's not that you don't want to—it's that no one's ever shown you what that looks like.

Here's what I had to learn: God doesn't live in the building you visit on Sundays. He's not confined to the worship songs or youth group pizza nights. He doesn't wait in the sanctuary while you live the rest of your life. He walks with you—into math class, into your family drama, into your DMs and your doubts.

"Never will I leave you; never will I forsake you." — Hebrews 13:5. That's not a Sunday promise—it's an everyday one.

Faith isn't a church service. It's a way of living. And it's not always loud or flashy. It doesn't always come with perfect words or a rush of emotion during worship. Real faith shows up in the quiet, ordinary, even awkward parts of life—the in-between moments no one posts about.

"Trust in the Lord with all your heart and lean not on your own understanding." — Proverbs 3:5. God doesn't ask you to figure everything out before you follow Him. He just asks you to trust Him in the middle of whatever today looks like.

"The righteous will live by faith." — Romans 1:17. Faith isn't just believing something in your head—it's about living it out with your

choices. It's a daily walk, step by step, trusting that God is real and present.

"So whether you eat or drink or whatever you do, do it all for the glory of God." — 1 Corinthians 10:31. That means math homework. That means lunch with friends. That means scrolling Instagram. Faith isn't a performance—it's about trusting God enough to let Him be part of your actual life, mess and all.

Caleb didn't grow up in a "church family." No memory verses taped to the fridge. No worn Bible sitting on the coffee table. No prayer before meals except maybe on Thanksgiving when someone's grandma insisted. For Caleb, weekends were for sleeping in, gaming, or hanging out with friends. Church wasn't even on the radar.

So when a friend invited him to youth group, he almost laughed it off. In his mind, church was for people who had their lives together—people who wore khakis, smiled too much, and spoke in a language he didn't understand. He pictured perfect kids pretending they never messed up, singing weird songs, and nodding along while someone lectured them.

Still... for some reason he couldn't explain, he showed up.

The first thing he noticed when he walked in wasn't the music—it was the noise. The room was alive. People were laughing, tossing a football, playing ping pong, hugging like they'd known each other forever. Nobody seemed as stiff or fake as he'd imagined.

Then the music started. A few kids raised their hands while they sang. Others closed their eyes. Caleb stood there awkwardly, hands stuffed in his hoodie pocket, trying to look like he wasn't completely out of place.

And then came the part he'd been dreading. The speaker said, "Turn to Philippians." Caleb froze. Was that in the front of the Bible? The back? Somewhere in the middle? He didn't have a clue. His heart pounded, his cheeks burned. He just opened to a random page and acted like he was reading along.

Everything about the night felt foreign. Unfamiliar. A little uncomfortable.

But then something happened.

Right before they split into small groups, one of the leaders prayed out loud and said, *"God, You're welcome in our mess."*

Caleb's chest tightened. That line hit different. Mess? He had plenty—arguments at home, grades slipping, a best friend who'd stopped talking to him, and a knot of anxiety that wouldn't go away. He didn't think God would want anything to do with that side of his life.

Later that night, lying in bed, he found himself thinking about that prayer. Almost without realizing it, he whispered in his head, *God... if You're real... I need You. Like, now.*

Nothing magical happened. No flash of light. No warm fuzzy feeling. But something small shifted.

Over the next few weeks, he kept showing up. At first, it was just because his friend asked him to. But slowly, he started listening—really listening. He asked questions. Not to sound smart or challenge the leaders, but because he actually wanted to know. He started praying—not long, impressive prayers, but quick, honest ones. And sometimes, before school, he'd read just one verse.

One day, when someone asked why he seemed more calm lately, Caleb shrugged and said, *"I think I'm starting to believe that God's actually with me. Like... for real."*

That's the thing—his faith didn't start with knowing all the answers or having a perfect church background. It started with honesty. It started when he stopped leaving God at the church door and started inviting Him into the messy, normal, in-between parts of his life.

So how do you live like faith matters—even when the weekend's over? You start small, and you start real.

You don't have to overhaul your entire life in one week. Nobody's expecting you to turn into a walking Bible app overnight. But you can take steps that move your faith from something you "do" at church to something you live wherever you are.

It's about inviting God into the moments you usually don't think about. The bus rides. The locker room. The quiet moments before bed. Even the awkward conversations where you're not sure what to say.

It might look like saying a one-line prayer before first period: *God, help me stay calm today.* Or whispering, *I need You,* before you walk into a tough situation. It might look like taking your earbuds out long enough to listen when someone needs to talk.

Faith is not about pretending you're perfect—it's about letting God be part of your actual, unfiltered life. That means you can be honest with Him when you're tired, stressed, confused, or even mad. He's not shocked by your feelings. You're not going to scare Him away.

Living by faith will sometimes make you stand out—and that can feel uncomfortable. You might be the one who doesn't laugh at a cruel joke, or the one who chooses not to cheat on an assignment. People might notice, and they might not always get it. But the point isn't to impress them—it's to follow the One who's walking with you.

When your faith moves into your everyday life, it stops being a performance and starts becoming a relationship. You're not just showing up to a service—you're showing up to life with God beside you. And the more you practice it in small ways, the more natural it becomes when the big moments come.

Yeah, bringing your faith into Monday can feel uncomfortable. Yeah, you might worry what people will think. But there's also the chance that your everyday faith—quiet, steady, real—will speak louder than any sermon you could preach. And that's worth it.

Here are some simple steps you can try this week:

- **Say one short prayer before school starts.** Something simple like, *God, help me see You today.* It's less about perfect words and more about inviting Him in from the start.
- **Carry one verse with you all day.** Write it on a sticky note, put it in your locker, or set it as your phone wallpaper. Let it pop up when you need it most.
- **Make one decision that lines up with your faith.** Refuse to join in on gossip. Tell the truth when lying would be easier. Choose kindness when sarcasm would get a laugh.

- **Look for one person you can encourage.** A quick "You crushed it today" or "Glad you're here" can go farther than you think.

- **Swap out one habit for a faith-building one.** Play worship music while you get ready. Read a Psalm before bed instead of scrolling.

You don't have to become a "super-Christian" overnight. You don't have to make every moment a spiritual highlight. All it takes is one small, honest step toward God, and then another.

Even if it feels like no one else notices, **God notices.**

You don't have to wait for the next *big* worship night or church event to feel close to God. You don't have to wait until you *"feel ready"* or until life magically settles down. **Faith is built in the normal, messy, in-between days**—when you decide to trust Him even when you're tired, distracted, or unsure.

Some days you'll feel bold. Other days you'll feel quiet. And that's okay. **God's not grading you on how loud or emotional your faith looks**—He's looking at whether you keep showing up.

And here's the thing—**when you keep showing up, even in the smallest ways, your faith starts to grow roots.** The kind that holds steady when the wind picks up. The kind that doesn't get shaken just because the day feels boring or someone questions what you believe.

So tomorrow, when you step into school, practice, or whatever's ahead—walk in like you're *not* alone. Because you're not. **God's already there.** He's in the hallway before you get there. He's in the conversation before you speak. **He's in the problem before you see the solution.**

You don't have to make Him fit into your schedule—**He's already in it.** You just have to notice.

So, take the next step. *Say the short prayer. Carry the verse. Choose the higher road.* Let God walk with you into all of it—**Mondays, Wednesdays, Fridays, and every ordinary, in-between day.** Faith in the everyday starts with one thing you probably haven't done enough of yet. Let's talk about it.

Real Talk Mantra: ***Faith isn't just for church—it's for every moment where you choose to walk with God, right where you are.***

Chapter Twelve

Real Guys Pray (Even If They Don't Know How)

Talking to God doesn't have to be weird. It's real—and it matters.

I used to think prayer was only for church people—the ones who always had the right words. You know the type. They'd bow their heads and suddenly turn into spiritual poets, saying things like *"Father God"* over and over, sounding like they had rehearsed in front of a mirror. Meanwhile, I'd keep my head down, fiddle with my shoelaces, and silently pray someone else would go first.

It wasn't that I didn't believe in God. I just didn't know how to talk to Him. *What if I said something wrong? What if I messed it up? What if everyone around me could tell I was faking it?*

One night, a friend was going through something heavy. The kind of stuff that makes your chest feel tight because you don't know what to do or say. He wasn't okay—and honestly, neither was I. So, I whispered three words: *"God, help him."* That's it. **No perfect sentence. No polished tone. Just honesty. Raw, shaky, real.**

And it hit me—**maybe that was enough.** Maybe prayer wasn't about saying it right. Maybe it was about showing up, even when I didn't know what to say. That simple whisper changed the way I saw everything.

Because prayer? **It isn't about performance. It's about connection.**

We make it more complicated than it needs to be. We think we need a script, a spiritual voice, the perfect time, or the right kind of day. **But God isn't looking for a show. He's looking for your heart.**

You don't have to fake it. You don't have to sound like anyone else. You don't even have to know what you're doing. **He's not grading your words. He's listening for your honesty.**

The truth is that prayer is less like a performance and more like a text to someone who's already in the room. It doesn't have to be long. It doesn't have to be the right words. It just has to be real. You don't have to wait until you feel *worthy* to pray. That's one of the biggest lies we believe that we have to be clean, polished, and put together before we can even talk to God. But that's backwards. **Jesus didn't come for people who had everything together. He came for the broken, the messy, the ones who needed help.** He came for you.

"But God has surely listened and has heard my prayer. Praise be to God, who has not rejected my prayer or withheld his love from me!" — Psalm 66:19–20. **God doesn't reject your prayers.** Not when they're short. Not when they're awkward. Not even when you're not sure you believe He's listening. Every time you speak, **He leans in like you're the only one in the room.** He takes every word seriously and responds with love—every single time.

"Come near to God and He will come near to you." — James 4:8. That means you don't have to figure out how to *get to* Him—you just have to turn toward Him. Whisper a sentence in the middle of math class. Say *"thank you"* before you fall asleep. **When you take even the smallest step toward Him, He's already moving faster toward you.** You'll never find Him with His arms crossed, waiting for you to measure up.

"Let us then approach God's throne of grace with confidence, so that we may receive mercy and find grace to help us in our time of need." — Hebrews 4:16. God's throne isn't a courtroom waiting to hand down a sentence. **It's a safe place.** A place where your worst moments aren't met with punishment, but with mercy. **You can come to Him exactly as you are, and you'll always be met with open arms.**

That's the heart of prayer. It's not a performance or a perfect script. **It's a real conversation with the God who already knows you—and still wants to hear from you.**

Marcus didn't grow up in a family that prayed. At dinner, there were no bowed heads. At night, no bedtime prayers. Church was something other people did. For him, God felt like a distant figure—maybe real, but not someone he actually knew.

He liked staying in the background. He wasn't the loud guy in class. He didn't raise his hand in youth group or lead worship or pray out loud. He listened more than he talked, and when he felt things, he felt them deep.

But everything changed the week his mom got sick.

He remembers the hospital like it was a different world—the sterile smell, the endless beep of machines, the harsh fluorescent lights that never seemed to turn off. His mom lay there, pale and quiet, connected to tubes and wires that made him nervous. The doctors spoke softly, but Marcus barely heard them. All he could focus on was the fear that gripped his chest.

It sat heavy, like a weight pressing down on his ribs. His hands felt clammy, and he shoved them into his hoodie pocket so no one would notice. The steady hum of the machines was the only sound he could hear.

He didn't know what to say. To the doctors. To his dad. To anyone. So, he sat in the quiet, barely breathing, and whispered, *"God... please help her."*

No lightning flashed. No miracle moment. No instant relief.

But something shifted in his chest—just enough to take one deep breath. That whisper—shaky and unsure—felt like the most honest thing he'd ever said.

He wasn't trying to be spiritual. He wasn't even sure if he believed it would work.

But in that moment, **God became more than a distant idea.**

He became the one person Marcus knew he could talk to—even if he didn't know what to say.

That week, Marcus kept praying. One line at a *time. "Thank You." "Be with her." "Help me not fall apart."*

The more he whispered, the less weird it felt.

It wasn't about confidence. It was about honesty.

And that's when he discovered the truth: **You don't have to be loud to be heard. You just have to be real.**

If prayer still feels awkward to you, you're not alone. And you're not doing it wrong. **You're learning to talk to the God who already knows you—and still wants to hear from you.**

Here's one way to start building a real prayer habit in your everyday life. It's not about perfection. It's about practice. And it's about being honest.

- **Pause before you scroll.** First thing in the morning, before your fingers unlock your phone—take a moment. Whisper, "God, I'm here. Help me today." That one simple sentence can shift your whole morning.

- **Pray one sentence today.** Anywhere—hallway, lunch table, practice. Say something real like, "God, help me breathe," or "I'm stressed, be near." Keep it short, honest, and from the heart.

- **Set a reminder.** Use a sticky note on your mirror or change your phone wallpaper to a simple prayer. Let that visual pull your attention toward God, even if just for a moment.

- **Write a note to God.** Type a sentence in your phone or scribble a thought in your notebook. "Here's what I'm thinking about." That's a prayer too.

Marcus didn't have a framework that night. He didn't need one. But as you grow, here's something simple that can help when you don't know where to start.

Try the P.R.A.Y. method when you feel stuck or don't know what to say:

- **P – Praise:** Start by telling God something you're grateful for. It could be as simple as *"Thanks for this new day"* or *"Thank You for my family."* Praising God helps you remember who He is and shifts your focus from your worries to His goodness.

- **R – Repent:** This means being honest about where you've messed up or hurt someone. It's not about beating yourself up, but about saying, *"I'm sorry for how I acted,"* or *"Please help me do better."* Repentance clears the way for a fresh start and reminds you that **God's grace is bigger than any mistake.**

- **A – Ask:** This is the part where you bring your needs and the needs of others to God. You can ask for help with school, courage to face a challenge, healing for a friend, or peace when things feel messy. **Asking shows you trust God to be part of your life and your problems.**

- **Y – Yield:** This means giving God control and trusting Him, even when you don't understand what's happening. It's saying, *"I don't know what the future holds, but I'm choosing to trust You."* Yielding isn't always easy—it's a daily choice to hand over your worries and fears to God and believe He's working even when you can't see it.

You don't have to say all four every time you pray. Sometimes, your prayer might just be one part—maybe a quick *"Thank You"* or a simple *"Help me."* Other times, you might say all four parts slowly, really thinking about each one.

The P.R.A.Y. method is just a tool to help you get started, especially when prayer feels hard or confusing. **It's not a test or a formula to get right.** It's more like training wheels on a bike—something to help you build confidence and keep moving forward.

Remember, prayer is a conversation, not a checklist. The important thing is **showing up and being real with God, no matter what your words sound like.**

The more you practice praying—even if it's just a little each day—the more you'll start to notice something amazing: **prayer changes you.** It doesn't just change your words or your mood; it changes your heart.

Prayer is how you build a relationship with God, just like any friendship. It takes time, honesty, and sticking with it even when it feels awkward or quiet. Sometimes, you'll feel like you're talking to yourself. Other times, you'll feel God's peace settle over you like a warm blanket.

And here's the best part: **God never gets bored or tired of hearing from you.** Every prayer matters to Him, even the ones you don't think count.

So don't give up. **Keep showing up. Keep being real. Keep trusting that God hears you and loves you, no matter what.**

You're already farther than you think—just by reading this and thinking about prayer, you're taking steps on a journey that lasts a lifetime.

You don't need a stage. You don't need a crowd. You don't need perfect words.

You just need a moment.

God's already near. He's already listening. And that quiet whisper—the one no one else hears? He hears it like thunder.

So talk to Him. About anything. About everything. About what makes you smile and what makes you want to break down. **He's not distant. He's not bored. He's not waiting for the "better" version of you.**

He's just waiting for you to open up. You've made it through twelve chapters. You're not the same guy who opened this book. Keep going.

Real Talk Mantra: ***Prayer isn't polished—it's honest. And God hears it.***

Part 3 Recap: Becoming the Guy God Made You to Be

Living with Character, Courage, and Real Faith

Take a breath. This part of the journey wasn't about pressure to perform or pretend. It was about learning how to live with *purpose*—even when life feels confusing.

You've seen that real strength isn't about muscles or image. **It's about character.** It's the quiet choices, the honest moments, the integrity that shows up when no one else is watching.

You've learned that courage isn't about being fearless. **It's about trusting God enough to take the next step**—even when your heart's pounding and your hands are shaking.

You've seen that faith doesn't have to sound impressive. It doesn't have to be loud or polished. Sometimes it's just one whispered sentence: *"God, I need You."* And that's enough.

You've explored what it really means to be a man—not the shallow version the world throws at you, but the kind rooted in something deeper: **Character. Courage. Real faith.** The stuff that actually lasts.

And maybe the biggest thing you've learned? **You don't have to have it all figured out.** God isn't looking for perfect—He's looking for honest. For real. For someone who's willing to show up, even when it's hard.

So if you're wondering who you're becoming... start here:

- *Be honest.*
- *Be brave.*
- *Be real.*

And take the next small step. God's not in a hurry. He's not disappointed. He's walking with you—one moment, one choice, one prayer at a time.

Keep going. You're becoming the guy He made you to be.

Conclusion: You've Got What It Takes — Now Keep Going

Let's be real—life doesn't follow a script. It zigs when you expect it to zag. Some days you feel strong; other days, you're just trying to keep your head up. But here's the truth—**right here, right now—you've come a long way.**

You've faced the mirror with honesty. You've named lies and fought back with truth. You've stepped into hard emotions instead of hiding from them. You've asked big questions about who you are, what you believe, and where you're going.

You've started building something real—a life rooted in *truth*, not pressure.

You've learned that your worth doesn't come from popularity or performance. **You've seen that emotions aren't weakness. Messing up doesn't disqualify you.** God's love isn't based on how well you hold it together—it's based on who He is. *And He's not letting go.*

You've picked up tools that matter. You've learned how to face anxiety, name shame, and walk through fear. You've figured out how to take ownership after failure, how to rebuild connection when things break, how to find peace in lonely moments, and how to stand strong when the pressure hits.

And maybe most importantly—you've realized you're not in this alone. **Not now. Not ever.**

So, when you hit that next wall—when the mirror starts to feel blurry, when fear gets loud again, when you wonder if you're really enough—come back to what's *true.*

You've got what it takes. **Not because you're flawless, but because the One who made you is still with you.** And He's not done writing your story.

So, keep going. *Keep growing.* **Keep showing up.**

You're not finished. You're becoming the man God made you to be.

You don't have to have it all figured out. You just have to take the next step. God's already in every one of them, and He's not done with the guy He made you to be.

Resources: Free Tools to Help You Grow

Free Tools to Help You Keep Growing

This journey doesn't end on the last page.

There are free companion tools you can download reflection pages, Scripture cards, and practical resources to help you live this out in real life.

Get everything at ivoryroad.shop

The Real Talk Series

If this book helped, there's more where it came from.

The **Real Talk Workbook** takes every chapter deeper. It's for the guys who are ready to stop pretending and start growing.

The **Real Talk Parent Guide** is designed for your parents. It helps parents understand what teenage guys are really carrying and how to walk alongside them without adding pressure.

The **Real Talk Leader Guide** is for youth leaders and mentors. Twelve fully developed sessions built for small groups, discipleship, and real conversation.

All four books work together. Each one stands on its own.

Sometimes the best thing you can do with hope is pass it on. Leave this book somewhere someone might need it. You never know who's carrying the same questions you are.

One Last Thing

You picked up this book for a reason. Don't put it down and move on like nothing happened. Take one thing from these pages and live it out this week.

The book is done. The work isn't. Let's keep going.

Scripture References

Chapter 1 – The Mirror Lies Sometimes

- **Psalm 139:14** – *"I praise you because I am fearfully and wonderfully made; your works are wonderful, I know that full well."*

- **Luke 12:7** – *"Indeed, the very hairs of your head are all numbered. Don't be afraid; you are worth more than many sparrows."*

- **Jeremiah 1:5** – *"Before I formed you in the womb I knew you, before you were born I set you apart; I appointed you as a prophet to the nations."*

Chapter 2 – I'm Not Like Everyone Else (And That's Good)

- **Romans 12:2** – *"Do not conform to the pattern of this world, but be transformed by the renewing of your mind. Then you will be able to test and approve what God's will is—his good, pleasing and perfect will."*

- **Job 10:8** – *"Your hands shaped me and made me. Will you now turn and destroy me?"*
- **Zephaniah 3:17** – *"The Lord your God is with you, the Mighty Warrior who saves. He will take great delight in you; in his love he will no longer rebuke you, but will rejoice over you with singing."*
- **Ephesians 2:10** – *"For we are God's handiwork, created in Christ Jesus to do good works, which God prepared in advance for us to do."*

Chapter 3 – Everyone's Faking It (Even the Confident Ones)

- **1 Samuel 16:7** – *"But the Lord said to Samuel, "Do not consider his appearance or his height, for I have rejected him. The Lord does not look at the things people look at. People look at the outward appearance, but the Lord looks at the heart."*
- **2 Corinthians 12:9** – *"But he said to me, "My grace is sufficient for you, for my power is made perfect in weakness." Therefore I will boast all the more gladly about my weaknesses, so that Christ's power may rest on me."*
- **Matthew 11:28** – *"Come to me, all you who are weary and burdened, and I will give you rest."*

Chapter 4 – What Does God Actually Think About Me?

- **1 John 3:1** – *"See what great love the Father has lavished on us, that we should be called children of God! And that is what we are! The reason the world does not know us is that it did not know him."*

- **Psalm 34:18** – *"The Lord is close to the brokenhearted and saves those who are crushed in spirit."*

- **Jeremiah 31:3** – *"The Lord appeared to us in the past, saying: "I have loved you with an everlasting love; I have drawn you with unfailing kindness."*

- **Romans 8:1** – *"Therefore, there is now no condemnation for those who are in Christ Jesus."*

Chapter 5: The Anger, the Shame, and the Ugly Cry

- **John 11:35** – *"Jesus wept."*

- **1 Peter 5:7** – *"Cast all your anxiety on Him because He cares for you."*

- **Psalm 34:18** – *"The Lord is close to the brokenhearted and saves those who are crushed in spirit."*

- **Psalm 62:8** – *"Trust in Him at all times, you people; pour out your hearts to Him, for God is our refuge."*

Chapter 6: I Messed Up. Now What?

- **1 John 1:9** – *"If we confess our sins, he is faithful and just and will forgive us our sins and purify us from all unrighteousness."*
- **2 Corinthians 5:17** – *"Therefore, if anyone is in Christ, the new creation has come: The old has gone, the new is here!"*
- **2 Corinthians 12:9** – *"But he said to me, 'My grace is sufficient for you, for my power is made perfect in weakness.' Therefore I will boast all the more gladly about my weaknesses, so that Christ's power may rest on me."*

Chapter 7: People Are Hard (But Worth It)

- **Romans 12:18** – *"If it is possible, as far as it depends on you, live at peace with everyone."*
- **James 1:19** – *"My dear brothers and sisters, take note of this: Everyone should be quick to listen, slow to speak and slow to become angry."*
- **Proverbs 17:17** – *"A friend loves at all times, and a brother is born for a time of adversity."*

Chapter 8: When You Feel Alone (Even in a Crowd)

- **Psalm 27:10** – *"Though my father and mother forsake me, the Lord will receive me."*
- **Matthew 28:20** – *"And surely I am with you always, to the very end of the age."*
- **Psalm 34:18** – *"The Lord is close to the brokenhearted and saves those who are crushed in spirit."*

Chapter 9: What Makes a Man (Hint: It's Not Muscles)

- **Joshua 1:9** – *"Have I not commanded you? Be strong and courageous. Do not be afraid; do not be discouraged, for the Lord your God will be with you wherever you go."*
- **Jeremiah 17:10** – *"I the Lord search the heart and examine the mind, to reward each person according to their conduct, according to what their deeds deserve."*
- **Psalm 73:26** – *"My flesh and my heart may fail, but God is the strength of my heart and my portion forever."*

Chapter 10: Doing Hard Things, Even When You're Scared

- **Isaiah 41:10** – *"So do not fear, for I am with you; do not be dismayed, for I am your God. I will strengthen you and help you; I will uphold you with my righteous right hand."*

- **Psalm 56:3** – *"When I am afraid, I put my trust in you."*

- **2 Timothy 1:7** – *"For the Spirit God gave us does not make us timid, but gives us power, love and self-discipline."*

Chapter 11: Faith Isn't Just for Sundays

- **Proverbs 3:5** – *"Trust in the Lord with all your heart and lean not on your own understanding."*

- **Romans 1:17** – *"For in the gospel the righteousness of God is revealed—a righteousness that is by faith from first to last, just as it is written: 'The righteous will live by faith.'"*

- **Hebrews 13:5** – *"Keep your lives free from the love of money and be content with what you have, because God has said, "Never will I leave you; never will I forsake you."*

- **1 Corinthians 10:31** – *"So whether you eat or drink or whatever you do, do it all for the glory of God."*

Chapter 12: Real Guys Pray (Even If They Don't Know How)

- **Psalm 66:19–20** – *"But God has surely listened and has heard my prayer. Praise be to God, who has not rejected my prayer or withheld his love from me!"*
- **James 4:8** – *"Come near to God and he will come near to you. Wash your hands, you sinners, and purify your hearts, you double-minded."*
- **Hebrews 4:16** – *"Let us then approach God's throne of grace with confidence, so that we may receive mercy and find grace to help us in our time of need."*

Real Talk Mantras

Chapter 1 – The Mirror Lies Sometimes
The mirror doesn't define you. God does.

Chapter 2 – I'm Not Like Everyone Else (And That's Good)
You weren't made to fit in. You were made to reflect Him.

Chapter 3 – Everyone's Faking It (Even the Confident Ones)
You don't have to fake strength to be confident. Real confidence comes from being real.

Chapter 4 – What Does God Actually Think About Me?
God sees the real me, calls me His masterpiece, and He's not walking away.

Chapter 5 – The Anger, the Shame, and the Ugly Cry
I don't have to hide how I feel to be strong. God sees the real me—and He stays.

Chapter 6 – I Messed Up. Now What?
God's grace is bigger than my guilt—and it's never too late to start again.

Chapter 7 – People Are Hard (But Worth It)
People are hard—but God gives me grace to love anyway.

Chapter 8 – When You Feel Alone (Even in a Crowd)
I am seen by God, loved as I am, and never truly alone. One honest step is enough to begin again.

Chapter 9 – What Makes a Man (Hint: It's Not Muscles)
Real strength isn't loud—it's built in the quiet, honest choices that reflect God's heart.

Chapter 10 – Doing Hard Things, Even When You're Scared
Courage isn't the absence of fear—it's trusting God enough to take the next step anyway.

Chapter 11 – Faith Isn't Just for Sundays
Faith isn't just for church—it's for every moment where you choose to walk with God, right where you are.

Chapter 12 – Real Guys Pray (Even If They Don't Know How)
Prayer isn't polished—it's honest. And God hears it.

About the Author

Dr. Scott Fuller has spent his life helping people grow through faith, leadership, and the kind of honest conversations that usually start with, "Let's be real."

With a doctorate in education and degrees in management and educational leadership, Scott brings both professional depth and personal experience to everything he creates. He has served as a junior high pastor, and in administrative roles such as Chief Financial Officer and Chief of Staff, positions that gave him a front-row seat to what it looks like when young people thrive and when they struggle.

As a longtime nonprofit leader, Scott has mentored young leaders, guided organizations, and helped build systems that serve thousands of students and families every day.

But it is his experience as a dad, a believer, and someone who has wrestled with insecurity himself that drove him to create Real Talk. He wrote it for guys who are tired of pretending and ready to become who God made them to be.

Scott believes that school, faith, and life do not have to be things you just survive. With the right tools and honest conversations, they can become a launching pad for real confidence, the kind rooted in something deeper than popularity or opinion.

His favorite titles? Husband. Father. Grandfather.

One Last Ask

You made it through. That matters.

If this book helped you feel less alone, think differently, or take even one step forward, would you leave a quick review on Amazon?

It doesn't have to be long. One honest sentence might help another guy pick up this book when he needs it most.

Thanks for being here. Keep going.

www.ingramcontent.com/pod-product-compliance
Lightning Source LLC
LaVergne TN
LVHW010838120826
845149LV00017B/3298
9781970494051